AF471191

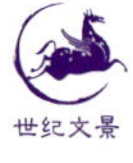

北京世纪文景文化传播有限责任公司 出品

沈远：急促的话语

SHEN YUAN: HURRIED WORDS

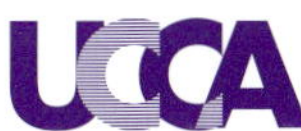

尤伦斯当代艺术中心 一石文化 编

世纪出版集团 上海人民出版社

馆长：杰罗姆·桑斯
Director: Jérôme Sans

策展人：郭晓彦
Curator: Guo Xiaoyan

主办单位：尤伦斯当代艺术中心
This exhibition is hosted by Ullens Center for Contemporary Art

展览时间：2009 年 5 月 16 日至 2009 年 7 月 18 日
Exhibition Period: May 16, 2009 – Jul 18, 2009

展览地点：尤伦斯当代艺术中心
Exhibition Venue: Ullens Center for Contemporary Art

北京市朝阳区酒仙桥路 4 号大山子艺术区（798 厂内）
798 Art District, No.4 Jiuxianqiao Lu, Chaoyang District, Beijing

《沈远：急促的话语》
Shen Yuan: Hurried Words

统筹策划：一石文化
Project Planning: ISreading Culture

编辑：史建　马健全　崔峤　陈韵　张铎
Editors: Shi Jian, Ma Kin Chuen, Cui Qiao, Chen Yun, Zhang Duo

翻译：杨思思　田霏宇
Translators: Yang Sisi, Philip Tinari

英文编校：Michelle Woo
English Editor: Michelle Woo

展览摄影：孙健伟
Exhibition Photography: Sun Jianwei

平面设计：吐毛球 @ 夏宇 & 广煜
Graphic Design: TOMEETYOU@XY&GY

特别鸣谢：Kamel Mennour 画廊
Special Thanks to: Galerie Kamel Mennour

目录

Contents

迁徙的身份：对沈远的访谈

The Migrating Identity: In Conversation with Shen Yuan

杰罗姆·桑斯
尤伦斯当代艺术中心馆长

JÉRÔME SANS
Director,
Ullens Center for Contemporary Art

杰罗姆·桑斯：1980年代晚期你和"厦门达达"运动的关系如何？

沈远：我只是个旁证人，并没有真正加入这场运动。我始终是独自工作的，我和永砅都希望在工作上尽可能地保持独立性，都可以成为对方的助手，但并不参与对方的工作，我想说的是创作和思考上的独立性。

杰罗姆·桑斯：你当时的作品是怎样的？

沈远：1980年代初我是一个在当时还很传统的浙江美术学院国画系的学生，所以花了点时间才让自己从中走出来。最初还是在纸上作各种反传统的尝试，直到有一天意识到它的局限性。当时我还在写作上作了一些实验，写了两三篇具有"新小说"风格的短篇小说，最后就干脆扔掉笔，拿起了榔头，就像你在尤伦斯当代艺术中心的展览"'85新潮"上看到的我的作品《水床》，我从平面走向三度空间。

杰罗姆·桑斯：你在1980年代移居法国，你的艺术创作反映了你的移民经历、语言的变化和文化的斗争。这个变化是否改变了你的思考和工作方式？

沈远：这次出国的经历对我是一次"冲击"，印象深刻。十六个小时的飞行之后，当你落地时一切准则全改变。我们那代人当时生活在一种完全封闭的状态，对外面的世界一无所知，因无备而有所击，有所击才有所感知。文化背景的完全改变，使我花了三四年的时间才明白自己所处的方位。这种背景的移位，使一些与生俱来的问题凸显："他者"、"身份"、"语言"。面对新问题自然改变了我的思考方式。当语言受阻时，艺术帮助我跨越了这一界限，所以在法国的最初阶段，我的作品中多次出现了舌头的形象，我借此象征着语言。在巴黎的第一件作品《白费口舌》是在一个私人的地下室，我做了九个冰制的舌头，它们从墙上和柱上伸出，各自的支撑物是把刀，舌融刀显，一个形象的转换。

杰罗姆·桑斯：你的作品《一个世界的早晨》重构了中国传统民居的屋顶，这是否是对你中国家乡的备忘录，并把它直接移植到西方美术馆的语境里？

沈远：我的作品常是我日常生活的一个片断，它曾在过去的某个时刻对我起过作用，在今天的某个机会我将它重现，在一个被更换的背景下，我以此隐喻一句我想说的话，并希望它重新对他人起作用。我成为一个创作者而不再是观看者。《一个世界的早晨》是在异地对家乡和童年的备忘录，这种备忘录就像这个传统房屋一样是自我封闭的，可见而不可触的。我喜欢移植一个情景，将过去的东西移到现场，又将现在的东西推向过去。这也像艺术本身，在距离中找回它的魅力。

杰罗姆·桑斯：这件作品是否像其他作品那样不仅包含了身份问题，同时也是对全球移民问题的具体呈现？

沈远：是的，我借着一个四壁无门的传统屋顶，来呈现移民问题：一个个对外封闭的群落，有趣地停留在某个"过去"的时段。就像在欧洲许多城市里的，中国城、意大利城、印度城、犹太城……有意地背离新环境，在"新空间"里凭着记忆建造一个个"旧空间"，这些"小空间"依附在"大空间"之下，却与它无关。我曾写过一段话："移民是背离一个空间，还是去占有另一个空间。我总是说我离开时那年代的母语，它改变了而我则停留着……"

杰罗姆·桑斯：在你的《黄色沙发》里，路易十五的椅子被中国传统布料覆盖。这是否是一种将西方／法国历史和中国相衔接的方式，用以逆转法国宏大历史叙事、中国历史或中国女性历史？

沈远：有句话："乞丐出门行李多。"一个移民的随身"文化行李"在"漂移"的过程中不断地黏合一身。在我的作品中也越来越多地出现多重文化为一体的现象。如《黄色沙发》正是我的生活背景的反映。另一个作品《不舒适的鞋》是由"三寸金莲"和"黑布鞋"构成一句话"Elles sont parties, pourtant elles n'ont nulle part où aller"（她们离家出走，却无处可去），来表达女权主义之后妇女的普遍处境。清代用裹脚的方式使妇女成为一个"物品"的概念，留守家中，毛泽东时代的"黑布鞋"则是另一个极端，女性非个性化——无审美，只是社会工具。我用这两个极端形式的"鞋"来写一句法文而非中文，使想说的问题不仅局限在中国的背景下，而是存在于今天妇女中的一个普遍性问题。

杰罗姆·桑斯：对你来说何处是家？

沈远：问一个渔夫："何处是家？"他会指着那条"船"；而问一个犹太人，他只能说："在脚下，何处不是家？"

杰罗姆·桑斯：你如何看待你在不同作品中涉及的两个世界间的桥梁形象？

沈远：移民为两地之间之物，既非我亦非彼，如"桥"。桥在建筑中跨度大，险而动（来来去去），如"移民"。我也喜欢使用与桥有关的材料：水和冰。不过我做的那些"桥"，都是些不可通过的桥。第一个桥是在荷兰的小城莱丹尔（Leerdam）的河上，《过河拆桥》是用当地工厂生产的啤酒瓶串接起来，并加上当地的玻璃回收桶构成的浮桥，只要过河之后一抽绳，桥便不复存在。另一个桥则是在西班牙的 NMAC 基金会的跑马场附近，此桥更类似于一个跑马场的障碍物，它由中国的青花瓷瓶和阿拉伯青瓷砖组合而成，扶手从桥上斜跨而过，使桥变得不可通。我想文化的作用不也亦然？

杰罗姆·桑斯：你是否认为你的作品和主题也和童年回忆有关？记忆对你来说意味着什么？

沈远：我在法国的一些早期作品中，出现了不少与回忆有关的主题，因为那时新的环境还没有真正与我产生关系，记忆就像大气层一样包裹着我。

杰罗姆·桑斯：你如何描述自己的作品？

沈远：最近我在卡枚·蒙鲁尔（Kamel Mennour）画廊的个展"空间的零度"，在开幕式的晚上，我将自己与观众之间的两扇门用大冰块封上，把我与观众隔绝开来，到第二天冰化之后我才出来。这是一种方式，艺术家拒绝交流和解释作品，而完全让作品自身说话。

杰罗姆·桑斯：你使用日常物品做作品很有名，从牛奶瓶子到奶嘴和温度计，为什么？

沈远：我始终不知道自己是不是真的算得上是一个专业"艺术家"，我从事艺术好像仅是我人生众多责任中的一个，不大也不小的责任。每天在排除了所有日常杂务之后，才可能理出一小块天地做点"艺术"，如果说我有众多的"职业"，那么"艺术家"是排名最后的；如果说这些日常琐事像空气一样围绕着我，那么在我的艺术中怎么可能没有它们？一个艺术作品的念头来得这么无法预计，可能在读书的过程中，也可能仅在触摸或观看一个物品的瞬间。

杰罗姆·桑斯：这是否是你所说的"艺术是种借尸还魂，揭露出事物的潜在语言，使得无用的东西变为有用，并使得有用的东西变为无用，这是我想要做的"？

沈远：我说过这句话，我想说的是人们给了艺术家一种"特权"，使他们可以不以世俗的价值观来判断事物，并给予事物以新的价值，这正是艺术家的责任所在。

杰罗姆·桑斯：你在 UCCA 的这个新展览为什么叫"急促的话语"？话语为何一定要快速急促？

沈远：速度即力量。言语也可获得势不可挡的动势。这就是为什么革命性的话语利用了口号式、命令式："打倒"、"胜利"、"低头"、"万岁"……短促的话语＝快捷的拳头。

杰罗姆·桑斯：在《急促的话语》这件作品中，80 个吹风机从天花板上悬挂下来，并定时、分别吞吐着布料做成的"舌头"，就像现在大众派对中所能看到的那样。为什么会出现带着舌头的吹风机？

沈远：舌头的形象多次在我的作品中出现，它与身体无关，却是"话语"的隐喻。使用吹风机吹舌是受启发于儿童时的玩具"小舌头"，此次是以机器代替人力。我第一次用吹风机是十年前，做了一个 12 米长的"歧舌"，一个高挂在三四米高的墙上的吹风机每四分钟吹一下这个舌头。它伸出时是对空间的侵犯，退缩时却是一种隐藏。歧舌——一舌两用，它时不时地发出吹气的轰轰声，可谓口齿不清，言不达意。这也是许多移民常有的言语窘境。而这次的80个吹风机同时吹出更如一场舌战，一场辩论会。吹风机的"热风"——"热语"。

杰罗姆·桑斯：在你的作品中有一种可以看得出的叙事能力，你通过各种日常生活的事物讲述"故事"。这次创作的《风景》，你是用我们日常生活中非常普通的"头梳"，这件东西很私人化，但在此，你将它呈现于一个公共的环境中。这些头发颜色不同，来自不同的文化背景，但却分享了同一把梳子。你是否在讲述把不同文化编织在一起的对话的必要性？

沈远：日常经验也常常是"共同"的，大同小异的，像工厂流水线上的产品，被每个人都触摸过，只有感受才是"私有"财产。我将它"私有化"后，再把这种也同样来自于流水线上的产品再次放回到公共空间——唤起共同经验。一个简单的生活细节：每天当我们梳理头发时，总有些发丝落在了梳子上，而这把梳子就像一把公用的梳子。在20世纪50—80年代的中国，所有的一切都是公共的：公共食堂、公共澡堂、公共厕所、公用茶杯、公用毛巾、公用厨房……没有私有财产。惟一私有的是"记忆"。这把梳子就像一个公共的物品，公用的空间，每个人都在上面留下了痕迹，它像一个人群或一个森林；不同的人种和物种在一个生存的公共空间里。

杰罗姆·桑斯：在巴黎卡枚·蒙鲁尔画廊的展览中，你有一个行为，将自己"冰封在"一个房间里，并在"被子"上绣出一些文字，这个行为与《急促的话语》这件作品有着密切的关系，是关于交流的。对于生活在"异乡"的人，离开了母语的环境，语言和交流成为问题。在你的作品中，通常这是一个反复出现的问题。能否请你深入谈一下？

沈远：由于语言上的"无能"而带来的被隔绝感，是我出国经验中最为深刻的一种体验。二十年过去了，也没有真正地从一种"静闭"的状态中走出来。因为当你没有一种自信与别人对话时，就只能进入一种"静闭"状态——思想的自我对话，自我循环。作品《空间的零度》可能正是这一状态的无意识的表露和有意识的自我隐退。冰将个人空间与公共空间隔离开来，我独自缝着句子："个人空间是稳定的，公共空间是浮动的，如果一个是宁静的，另一个则是骚动的；而一个感到不确定时，另一个则找回它的确定性……"这冰墙将融解，只是待何时？只有艺术是惟一的一种语言，可以冲破所有的文化界限。

杰罗姆·桑斯：你的作品中存在很多把日常物品放大的例子，譬如放大的梳子，放大的奶嘴，放大的温度计。为什么要放大这些东西的尺寸？你认为这是一种魔力还是一种诗意？

沈远：魔力和诗意是不可分的，前者是阳性，后者为阴性。而将一个可拿在手中的物品放大到接近建筑的尺寸，则更近乎魔力。我想当物品的尺寸改变之后，它的性质也随之改变。体温计——一根惟一可顺理成章地插入体内的小棍条，在变为三四米长时，它更像孙悟空的定海神针金箍棒。鱼在它的腹中游，它的游动变化着读数，而鱼自身的体温也随着水温的高低而改变。我以此比喻移民的善于适应环境的生存能力，所以作品题目为《变温动物》。我总是用身边触手可及的事与物，来达到以简入出的表达。

杰罗姆·桑斯：你如何看待今日的中国？作为一个中国女性艺术家，你有什么样的感觉？

沈远：今天的中国处在乱中取胜的年代。艺术界亦如此，没有什么游戏规则，也不想懂。这样就敢做，前无古人才后有来者。我每次做完一个作品都有遗憾，但一想我是个中国艺术家，又是女性艺术家，双重的不足，所以还可以再犯一次错……

沈远的词与物

Shen Yuan's Words and Objects

郭晓彦
尤伦斯当代艺术中心首席策展人

GUO XIAOYAN
Chief Curator,
Ullens Center for Contemporary Art

沈远 1959 年出生于中国福建省仙游市。1982 年毕业于浙江美术学院（现中国美术学院），1989 年参加中国美术馆的"中国现代艺术展"（通常称"89 大展"），第二年移居巴黎。其时，她最重要的作品《水床》，对当时的生命存在和政治形势进行了基于个人体认的分析和批判；在离开中国后，迁移带来的文化断裂和文化身份的确立，成为她的一个创作新起点，她的创作在文化身份、历史记忆和语言转义的复杂语境中展开。1990 年代，沈远在巴黎的工作受到关注并开始享誉国际。

沈远是中国当代艺术领域的一名卓有成就的女性艺术家；她的创作常游弋于日常生活的朴素的场景、语言隐喻及转换之中，在呈现大手笔和壮观场景的同时，浸入一种轻盈、细腻而深沉的特质，同时也透露出某种复杂信息和语义。在我们的现代经验中，人的可能性是在知识中创立的，这里包含着思想的一个律令，思想既是其所知的一切的知识，又是其修正；既是其反思对象——人的存在方式之反思，又是其转化。思想的目的在于必须使自身的存在发生改变，或者在非思的方向上行进，否则将无法发现"非思"。所以，"现代思想，一开始并且就其深度而言，就是某种行动方式"。人的他者（l'autre）应该成为与人相同者（le même）。正是在这里，福柯发现人处于一种权力内部，这个权力使人散开，使人远离他自己的起源；但这个权力不是别的，它就是人自己的存在的权利。所以，如果没有语言，没有词与物的关系的说明，我们将与世界无关，与历史无关，甚至在天地间也无从建立个人的存在之境。在呈现于我们面前的漫长的遗忘中，语言对于我们像是失而复得的"时间形象"，经由我们每个人身体（记忆）的通道，呈现在广阔的阅读的视野之中——个人经验像书写的痕迹，让个人和世界的边缘变得暧昧，从而使存在清晰起来。对于个人，语言不是思想，不是智慧，甚至不是真理，而是生命存在的"即兴的乐句"（罗兰·巴特）；而另一方面，语言又有着其承载的历史和幻想，经由语言，我们才能确定世界和自身的位置。

《白费口舌》（1994）是沈远 1994 年第一个国外（巴黎）的个展的作品，是她在异乡创作的，这是一件与（中国）语言有关的作品。在中国语言中，通常的意义上，"舌头"同时具有语言器官与肉体器官双重的意义，即它似乎同时具有生理和精神的象征性的双重特点。在中国成语中，"白费口舌"的意思亦是指谈话（交流）一无所获。这件作品的创作与她身处异乡遭遇"异样"的语言（存在），同时远离母语的精神经历有关，也与留存在记忆深处并被重新唤醒的对于词语暴力的警惕有关。在展览现场，几根巨大的、血红的冰舌头插在展场的大厅柱子上，"冰舌"随着时间慢慢融化，"口水"缓缓滴进下面的金属盆盂里，在冰舌融化的过程中，逐渐显露出深藏于冰舌中的锋利尖刀。沈远认为，"由于'舌头'这个词意味着言语字词，而融化着的冰舌表现出毫无限制地滥用语言，那么'舌头'意味着语言的流失。"并且，当舌头被赋予一种主动、复杂的功能时，它所携带的暴力也许会大过拳头的威力。《白费口舌》同时也与艺术家身处异邦而对母语（在此她使用的成语有着多重意味）在一个非母语环境里沟通"丧失"的细腻、深入的观察和思考有关。对于冰的材料的特性，沈远有自己的看法：它有刚性特征，更有柔性一面，细腻、敏感，犹如女人之心；而语言亦有细腻敏感的特性，它使交流变得可能，也有可能由于细微的差别而"差之毫厘，失之千里"。

在尤伦斯当代艺术中心展出的《急促的话语》，是艺术家于 2008 年在巴黎首展的新作，这也是一件关于语言，并与她以前的作品有着内在联系的作品。这件由 80 个吹风机构成的声音装置，吹风机"吹出来的风"会把它们那各种颜色画布的"舌头"拉直，并使其发出"急促而迅速的语言"。在这里，它们"说的话"既不可理解，又无法让他人倾听，显得噪音震耳——这是沈远的问题：脱离了丰富营养的母语的移民，在另一种语言里怎么保持言说的可能和能力？又怎样被这种想保有的语言隔绝和孤立在孤独之中？艺术家在思考因语言的失去、消失而变得空虚的同时，也深刻地揭示了语言对描述和翻译一些活生生的现实的功能局限性。与此同时，母语中坚硬的部分怎样消融以获得从另一种语言的词语中构成思考、反省和重新塑造自己的力量？

在巴黎"空间的零度"展览开幕的晚上，沈远走出人群，将自己置身于两块冰壁后面的房间里：在透明的阻隔的一侧，语言的记忆回响来自遥远的母语，但这些仿佛那些正在远离自己，变得歧义、闪烁不定的词汇。另一侧，她整夜在冰封的房间独自在被子上用生活之地的法语绣出正在思考的问题，比如，"艺术让我在空间和时间上跨越这些（语言）限制"，"移民的舌头就像蛇的舌头：被包裹着而且分叉。同一个舌头说出两种语言而且就像蛇发出嘶嘶声一样说不清楚"。这件作品里还蕴含着沈远一直关注和思考的问题：在文化混杂的现实中，我们能信任交流吗？对于自我生命的直接的感受如何能通过语言传达给"他者"，如何能直接向"他们"说出自身的经历，语言如何呈现不同语境中的可理解性、复杂性和可转义性？

沈远曾说，艺术家的职责就是"赋予物体信息"。如果她的愿望是给予无生命体以自己的舌头，那即是赋予它们一种使用现有的、多元的、口头或书面语言的沟通能力。然而，典型如其作品，这个愿望也同时表现了语言的独有性及局限性，也许是视觉才能将意义渗入到字句里面。"我的兴趣总是在于形象的转换，这也是我的作品的始发点……"沈远为尤伦斯当代艺术中心的展览创作的《风景》，与她的一系列关于头发的作品，包括 1996 年为在奥地利的展览"包容与排斥"创作的《三个沙发》（1996 年，格拉茨，奥地利）、《三五成群》（1997 年，卡姆登艺术中心，伦敦，英国）、《黄色沙发》（2001 年，阿尔隆非利，布里斯托尔，英国）有着某种联系，这是艺术家对于外在于身体之物的隐喻之意的系列沉思，可以说，对身体问题的思索即是其内在转变的需要。

《风景》这件作品用了头发作为"物"来说事。头发对于人，究竟意味什么？"头发和身体可以构成一个加减关系，头

发起源于身体，但是身体可以断然地减去它，身体可以视它为一个多余物或者剩余物。头发不构成身体的一个基本功能元素，它是无用的，因而也是廉价的；同时，头发还有倔强的绵绵不断的再生力，因而也绝非稀缺。此外，头发和身体的分离是一个没有苦痛的分离，既没有精神的苦痛，也没有肉体的苦痛。这种分离是安全的、平静的、非伤害性的，因而也是随处可见的、触手可及的和平淡无奇的。头发的起因是严格地依赖于身体的，而它的结构与身体则只有脆弱的若有若无的关联。"[1]

源于身体，又外在于身体的头发，既不是标记身体的性别沟壑，也不代表"主体"的本质，但它又在身体的文化身份和时代性中担当一种特有的含义，它的长短形状，是自我音容笑貌的外在特征和精神指向，具有特殊的象征性。头发的颜色曾经是中国人在与"他者"的历史交汇中认识"他者"的"思想"标志：黑色是"我们"特有的头发颜色，而黄色的、银色的、红色的等等则是属于"他人"的，在中国文化中曾对其他种族头发颜色给予谐谑甚至稍带贬义的称呼。但是在当今"染发"时代，对于颜色的任意改成为一种特有的心理征象，头发所代表的人的特质被物化为一种时代氛围，转变为对于世界一统造成的生存困境的压力及骚动不安的情绪。

在沈远的作品中，"头梳"上缠满着"不同的人"每天脱落的头发，这件人人熟悉的东西，在这里被转换成了一件不能明确定义其性质的"事物"，仿佛是生命的痕迹却又如此无生命感。在沈远的创作中，"物品"总是有着几重寓意，在看似随意的选择中常常"不经意"地流露着某种隐喻。物品所要关怀的是个体的历史观？对流逝生命和时间的生命、时光和记忆的描绘？或者也有其隐含其中的政治课题？——漂泊与语言，日益全球化的概念中的文化交流、翻译的可能性，语言与政治空间，等等。

沈远曾说，她希望通过揭示物体中潜在的语言，将无生命变为有生命，化腐朽为神奇，变有用为无用。她喜欢在作

品中显现那些物质的细枝末节，这些细微之处更细腻地表
达着作者的敏感心境，对生活和世界的见解。我们在展览
的两件作品中能够看到艺术家在记忆和沉思中缓缓前行的
细致体验和思考，以及她的作品特有的深刻而动人的气质。

1   汪民安，《身体、空间与后现代性》，江苏人民出版社，2006年，第68页。

从他者的语言到跨文化性

From Alien Language to Trans-Culturality

索珂·法依－瓦卡里
巴黎第八大学美学副教授

SOKO PHAY-VAKALIS
Associate Professor in Aesthetics,
The University of Paris VIII

在我们这个被打上历史悲剧、社会巨变以及政治和生态烙印的时代，移民艺术家在体现双重文化的同时，还在思索新的跨文化实践和多重身份的不同形式。自从 1990 年离开中国来到西方，沈远不断地开启有关文化交流共存的讨论。她见证着共存的文化之间缓慢而必要的相互作用，这些文化有时共存，有时互相渗透，有时相互借用。从这个意义上来说，她独特的作品，带有些许颠覆性讽刺的色彩，在全球文化重组过程中具有一种象征性；她的创造力粉碎了那些顽固的偏见，即所谓文明冲突的陈词滥调。[1] 她的装置作品超越了地域或民族的界限，结合了未经加工的和难以留存的材料，甚至活物，让我们体会初到异乡或开始跨文化体验时本能的不适。

向另一个自我的旅行

离开故土后，沈远用漂泊和语言及文化上的考验，锻造了她的思想和艺术，这艺术成为了今天的历史和社会经济现实的一部分。她知道从此动摇了的对故土的依恋有多深，背井离乡带来的冲击就有多突然和猛烈。[2] 一个她成长于其中的世界和语言退却了，并将她隔绝在孤独中。她长久地留存着对离开时的记忆和强烈印象，然后一生的时间都将用来思索离开的时刻，思索这种失去了什么、丢失了根和缺乏坐标的内心体验，因为生命至关重要的部分就蜷缩在这一时刻里。正如作品《一叶之舟》（2001 年）想要表达的。这只呈树叶形状的奇怪的小船很不结实，由几个绑在一起的铁锅组成，锅里盛满了食物、香料或是东方的烹饪材料。中国人无论走到哪里，总是离不开他们熟悉的味道，将其视若珍宝。用萨尔基斯的话来说就是："所有背井离乡的人都将文化背在背上。"[3] 这种前路茫茫的感觉——正像一片在水中漂流的树叶——又因为船上飘出的忧郁的歌声而愈发显得强烈：那是沈远在中国遇见的年轻的街头歌手杨一的歌声。他的歌里有相遇，有离开后试图在别处，在有时艰难而不稳定的条件下重建生活的人们的故事。所有向着别处的起程都是走向另一个自我的旅程。

2001 年《如鱼得水》在英国的布里斯托尔展览，这是个以蓝色玻璃器皿而闻名的城市。沈远通过该作品展现了船的主题的另一变化形式，强调了人被放逐时既是脆弱的，却又充满毅力和求生的力量。这个装置由一片白色的沙漠之海组成，其间散落着一只小船，一些鱼骨和蓝玻璃餐具，这些都是考古的"遗迹"，是旧世界的残迹。然而，小船里有一些鱼在一点点的水里游着。通过置换的游戏（海水变成了大片的盐）和带讽刺意味的旁观（"如鱼得水"），沈远揭示了创作和生活一样，既是不断的迁移，也是由放逐中永恒的回归。她搜集对地点和经验的记忆，却从不作长久的停留。她因一次相遇，一次"共同的感性体验"[4] 驻足，继而再次离开，从一地到另一地，不断得到充实。对成为游牧艺术家的她来说，无论是空间的还是语言的考验，都存在于两块土地上，因为没有回归的可能。事实上，故乡本身也仿佛渐渐带上了异乡的痕迹。

语言的变化

即使在法国 19 年了，沈远仍继续对语言和文化的"翻译"进行探索，由此质疑与他人之间的艰难而不确定的关系。比如她 2008 年秋在巴黎卡枚·蒙鲁尔画廊的展览和行为艺术《空间的零度》，是向罗兰·巴特的致敬。后者曾赞扬语言的精炼和形式的简单是诗歌以及政治的冲力所在。

开幕式当晚，沈远远离人群，在两堵冰墙之后，让人看不见，摸不着，身边只有几件简单的物品（一把木制扶手椅，一张桌子，一些线团和一条被单）。在冰墙两边形成鲜明对照的是两个不同的，不可重叠的世界：一边，是远远传来的人们的声音，听起来都是些不可辨认的只言片语；另一边，通过慢慢融化的冰墙显现出一个模糊的身影。还要等冰融化多久才能"打破僵局"？《空间的零度》表现的不仅是人们难以适应的温度刺激，还有对在展厅里与人交流的排斥，而类似的场所通常是用于人际交流和资金往来的。沈远把自己与世界的喧嚣隔绝开来，整夜都在被单上绣着不同的句子。比如，"移民，就是逃离一个空间，或者试图占据另一个空间。我仍然在说着我离开时的母语。它变了，我却依旧。艺术使我得以跨越时空的界限。"或者是，"外来移民的舌头就像蛇的舌头，卷曲而分叉。同一个舌头说着两种语言，就像蛇嘶嘶作响一样不能清晰表达"。

最后这句话使人联想起她的一个声效装置，即 80 个悬挂在天花板上的、电线长短不一的吹风机。装置以毫无规律的、分散的方式逐一接通吹风机的电源，风力使它们伸出各色布料作成的舌头。这些"短而促的语言"说得太多，最终枯竭，证实了理解的障碍和想让人听见的无力尝试，尽管它们的噪音震耳欲聋。

所有背井离乡的人都要经历语言被剥夺的那种痛苦，确切地说是因为语言赋予了人"存在的合理性"：我们自出生起就可以毫无保留地使用被称作"母语"的语言，用它来述说、描绘世界，因而这种语言应该是唾手可得的。但是，再没有比语言更复杂和封闭的体系了，它在没能有幸"生于其中"的人面前竖起了难以逾越的壁垒。这就是为什么要在别人的语言中获得任何话语的能力都需要思维的努力，以及重新组合和离乡后重新适应自我的努力。

沈远将这一语言被剥夺的体验做成了她最有力量的作品之一《白费口舌》，这个作品 1994 年在一个酒窖里展出。九个巨大的冰制舌头，最终融化成滴进痰盂里的水，露出它们的骨骼——巨大的尖刀。她借助"舌头"（langue）一词的多重含义来玩文字游戏，因为它既有作为交流手段的"语言"的意思，又是一个肉质的味觉和感官器官，同时它还具有矛盾的特性，其中暗含着隐喻（柔软、锐利、伤人），并由它衍生出一些习惯表达（根据中国的说法，"垂涎"）。这种从一个画面到另一个画面的转换——冰变成了一把危险的刀——使人联想到语言的变化。于是迁移时而是脱离人在一地扎根时被动接收的语言环境，时而是一种对语言力量的再创造，时而又变成对语言自主性的新发现。

二者之间的不适

背井离乡的人的语言和文化，既是地理上的位移，也是心理上的位移，通过对其继承的情感和文化传统的翻译，它们便获得更大的关注，更多的"认同"（更好的"再认识"）。在词源学上，"翻译"不正是"传递"的意思吗？从这个角度来看，沈远请每一个人都来体验词义的消失和转换。她那些奇特的桥，则暗指对所知的放弃和不确定而引起的不适[5]：无论这些桥是用回收玻璃瓶（1997 年的《过河拆桥》），还是用蓝色风景画点缀的中国青花瓷瓶和阿拉伯风格陶瓷（2004 年的《桥》）构成的，它们都不可能让人通过。穿越就如同在两岸之间"悬而不决"，象征移民在坚守故乡文化还是信奉迁居地的文化之间犹豫不决，由此体会到的痛苦和左右为难。这种"介于二者之间"的状态体现了在历史和文化的分离中，个人经历的矛盾性。

但是，不确定是一个西方文化惧怕的概念，它将阴暗和模糊归结为笨拙、误解和荒谬。尽管如此，对语言和文化的翻译正是在表达某种"完成不了的"、不确定的意思，因为翻译在两种文化间往返，呈现它们的差异，从而以另外的方式、节奏和色彩来表达世界。只有看到主体及其经历的历史与现实环境，才能让人理清真相。这就是为什么，即使有时差异是无法逾越的，但与他人的相遇必然是一种财富，是重要的主观体验。

于是沈远瓦解了我们的感官习惯和期待。通过这一既是分裂的又使人困惑的感官经历，沈远带我们体验了主体偏离中心地位，而主体在远离和同化之间的脆弱平衡[6]也不断地经历建构和解构。事实上，她无意通过融合远离和同化来解决或跨越二者之间的对立，而是寻求它们之间的"兼容"，这就需要对二者的"理解"，即将二者"共同拿起"（法文中"理解"[comprendre]一词由"共同"[com]和"拿起"[prendre]两部分组成。——译注）。尽管这种状态艰难且不稳定，建立在各种文化的不可还原性之上，但是它带来了一种动态的能量，使我们更关注那些独特的声音。

从这个角度来看，"思考外部"或"思考两者之间"将有可能引发距离和差异，并由此引入吉尔·德勒兹所定义的"变化"："不是一个概念成为另一个，而是每个概念都遇见另一个，是一种不同于两个概念的变化，因为它们之间毫无关联，但介于两者之间的，是一种变化，一种平行的演变，自有其方向。"[7]

不可翻译的部分

观看沈远的作品，我们有时会感到不理解和不适（尤其是她使用金鱼这样的活物），这是因为我们在看一种传达不同的美学观念和文化传统及习惯的艺术时，会体会到"异乡的考验"[8]。我们在对照别的语言和文化时遭遇的困难，可以用"考验"一词来归纳，因为它具有"忍耐"和"检验"的双重意义。从此，艺术家企图创造出将被两边同时看到、读到和听到的作品，并且，用保罗·里格尔的话说，碰撞到"不对等的相似"[9]这样一个矛盾。怎样使自己本源的文化变得奇怪？怎样在自我和他者之间建立起对话，而这个他者同时也是接纳我们的地方？

正是有了这种多元性的情结，对他者作品的诠释才能避免陷入单一化。而且，创作行为正处于不可翻译性的缝隙以及两种文化之间不确定的时间性的核心地带。从这方面来说，艺术家如同翻译者，希望同时存在忠实和背叛，既有某种保留又不排斥丢弃一些东西。放弃一种绝对的文化是必要的，这样才能接受辩证的距离，直到接受自身与他者之间不可逾越的差异。早在一个世纪以前，在《论异国情调》一书中，维克多·谢阁兰就明白了错误的抉择以及文化融合带来的风险，这种融合不过是另一种将文化占为己有或同化的方式："随着空间距离的大幅度缩短和障碍的消失，某处必然出现了新的隔阂和未知的空隙。"[10]

尽管文化翻译具有极大的颠覆性，它首先仍然是一种目标，一种远景，并根据变化、历史及文化社会前提的需要，随时接受重复的可能性。比如沈远的一件很美的作品《不舒适的鞋》，作品中上百双黑色小布鞋在一整面墙上跑开，有些略微触到地面。从远处我们可以看出，布鞋排列出的一句话："她们离家出走，却无处可去。"这些布鞋让人想起中国的不同时代：清代的审美标准强迫女人在很小的年纪就开始缠足；"文化大革命"统一了穿衣风格（不分年龄，同样的黑色）；然后终于到了我们这个移民潮涌动的时代，成千上万的女性为了更好的明天远离故土，却最终陷入孤独和贫苦。这件装置作品的轻巧和美好恰恰反衬出无尽的迁移和历史的悲剧。

混合中的新生

在作品《石腹》中，通过使用隐喻，沈远揭露了激进决策所造成的严重后果。这是一个巨大的石刻鱼缸，其中有一些五彩的鱼在游动，表现了三峡工程引发的问题。而在《仙游》中，她用一根绳子挂起一些巨幅照片，照片里的是她出生的村庄。可是如今的社会难以抗拒各种野心和对权力及财富的追逐，由此滋生的垃圾和废品侵占了村庄，将它变得面目全非。照片底下排列着一些回收材料制成的奇怪的家禽，踏在一长条干裂的土地上，这土地使人联想到枯竭了的古老语言……经济的过度增长并非治愈社会不平衡和不平等的良方。恰恰相反，这些剧烈的社会变动排斥了部分人口，使普通人或被全球化遗忘的人们的生活变得更加动荡、艰难了许多。为了维持生计，他们只能依靠自己，并且被迫不断地寻求新的收入来源。于是在中国南方省份，脚踏三轮车从城市景观中消失，让位于流动商贩的自行车。比如2008年在尤伦斯当代艺术中心展出的作品《触角》：三辆老式的三轮车已经废弃不用，任凭自行车取代它们，数量不断增加。但是它们之间是用铁链连着的，就像章鱼、水母和它们众多的触须。车夫不再搭载乘客，而是去向他们兜售餐具、扫帚、植物、鸟笼、驱蚊霜、玩具或是彩色气球。沈远对当代世界的变化尤为敏感，她让我们更注意文化间的传递，而非驻足于某一文化；更注重其翻译和转换的过程，而不是无谓的比对。

时值沈远在中国的首次个展在尤伦斯当代艺术中心举办，艺术家本人选择了一件混杂、沉淀了多重文化的作品，以此独特的方式来表达我们不断变化的、充满动荡的大都市：《风景》是一把长达 8 米的西式梳子（亚洲人更习惯用中式梳子），而这件西式梳子却是由中国传统的漆木制成。这件既普通又私人的物品，其外形隐约让人联想到一只船，或是我们的"大都市"的国际化。橙色的梳齿上缠绕纠结着头发，象征了丰富。近看的话，我们就能发觉执着于细节的沈远完成了一件了不起的作品，头发的种类繁多，既有不同的颜色、类型和年龄，甚至也有从最简单到最夸张的各种发型款式。在我们的文明中，头发象征了生命、诱惑、力量和权势，揭示了与他人的关系，如同权利或情感的标记。[11] 无论是顺直的、卷曲的、蓬松的、波浪形的、绑起来的，还是染过的、编好的头发，都见证了语言、文化和宗教的大量混合。

于是，旧的城市模式消失了，让位于新的现实。在其中一个梳齿上的是沈远复制的老家福州的地图，这与其说是出于思乡之情，不如说是展现对一个地方、一种血缘，以及用她父亲的头发做的发髻的情感记忆[12] 的全部重要性。记忆是过去和未来间的延续，在一个转变的世界里变得十分重要。"trans"（前缀，意为穿过，转换，变化。——译注）这个词缀的活力使观点的共享、对不同方式的感官和感觉的认同成为可能。《风景》表现的是霍米·巴巴极为强调的"（城市）第三空间"："全球和各民族文化的不同的时间性敞开了一个文化空间—— 一个第三空间，在这个空间里，无法估量的差异之间的协调为边缘者创造了独特的张力。"[13]

艺术的特性就在于这种"游戏"的能力，它能让有创造性的反常规取代既定的规矩、隔离的限制，它抓住关键，揭示矛盾，坚决抵制人们默认的同一化和身份诉求的封闭性。此外，在全球文化"重组"的情况下，这不是一种像"拼贴"那样将各种文化混合起来的混血艺术；而是在两种画面相

遇、文化间产生摩擦的空间里才能产生出某些东西。没有差距，也就没有创造形式的可能。

我们要创造的世界可能会更青睐"多元的差异"，即同时保留多种特有的文化。[14] 这就是为什么尝试放弃和偏离自我，将有可能接受异域的他者；这里并非将他者作为"征服"对象（否则会将主体置于"知识即权力"的立场），而是作为"发现"的对象。沈远正是在这样"乐观"的漂泊、不断的循环往来中，汲取跨文化的艺术灵感。在全球化时代，这样的艺术消解了东西方的严格对立，使人对社会、政治和生态的转变有了更进一步的理解。沈远完全没有强调她的中国艺术背景，而是不断地提供一个变化的空间，人人都可以在其中重新构建艺术和生活之间的可能。如今，关键在于定义一个文化或身份翻译的标准，其目标不再是囊括或同化他者（因为任何主体在其历史性中都是变化的），而是建立一种共存机制，使人们获得在平等和包容中保留差异性的权利。

（杨思思译）

1　见爱德华·W. 萨义德，《东方主义，西方创造的东方》（1978 年），巴黎，门槛出版社，2005年，第358页。

2　见施姆埃尔·特里加诺，《背井离乡的日子》（2001 年），帕约和里瓦热出版社，巴黎，2005 年，第 17 – 19 页。

3　见我的文章"记忆和忘却：萨尔基斯笔下的静默的形象"，《绝对艺术》，第5期，2003年6月，第38页。

4　我借用了雅克·朗希耶尔的说法，见《共同的感性、美学和政治》，巴黎，制造出版社，2000年。

5　见霍米·巴巴，《文化的场所》（1994年），巴黎，帕约出版社，2007年，第40 – 41页。

6　同上，第33页。

7　吉尔·德勒兹，《对话》，巴黎，弗拉马利翁出版社，1996 年，第 13 页。

8　安东尼·贝尔曼，《异乡的考验》，巴黎，伽俐玛出版社，1984 年，第 15 – 16 页。

9　保罗·里格尔，《翻译的挑战和幸福》，巴黎，拜亚出版社，2004 年，第 14 页。

10　维克多·谢阁兰，《论异国情调》，全集，巴黎，拉封出版社，1995 年，第 772 页。

11　见《头发》，菲利浦·慧林格，引自《象征物》，日内瓦，埃利沃出版社，1988 年。

12　沈远几次在作品中使用头发作为生活、记忆和孤独的象征，比如1996年的《三个沙发》，1997年的《三五成群》，2000年的《发屋》，以及最近2009年的《风景》。

13　霍米·巴巴，《文化的场所》，第 332 页。

14　弗朗索瓦·拉普朗第那，亚利克斯·努斯，《混血，从阿尔钦博托到幽灵》，巴黎，波维尔出版社，2001年，第224页。

作品

Works

风景
Landscape

2009年
装置
850×300×150 厘米

2009
Installation
850×300×150 cm

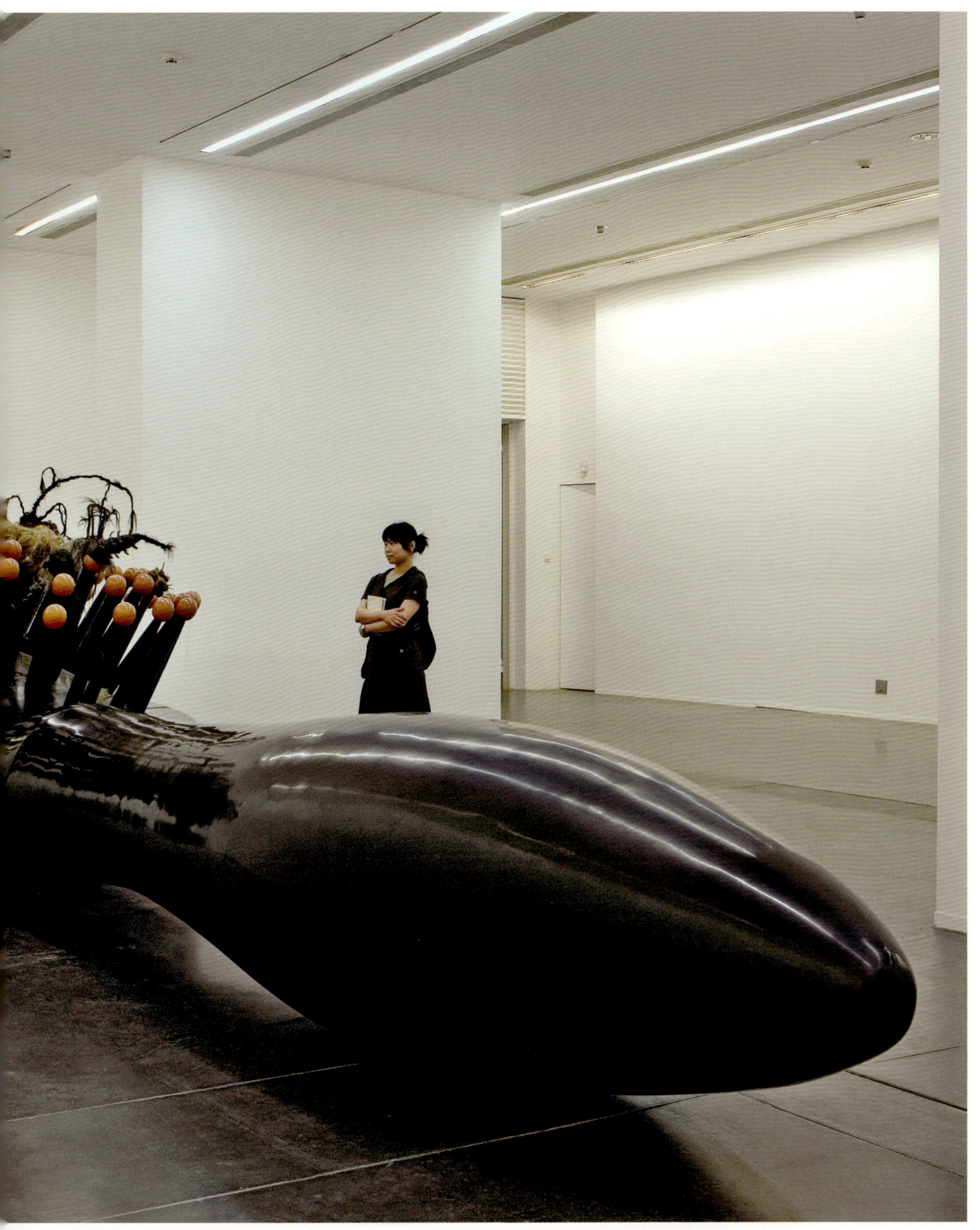

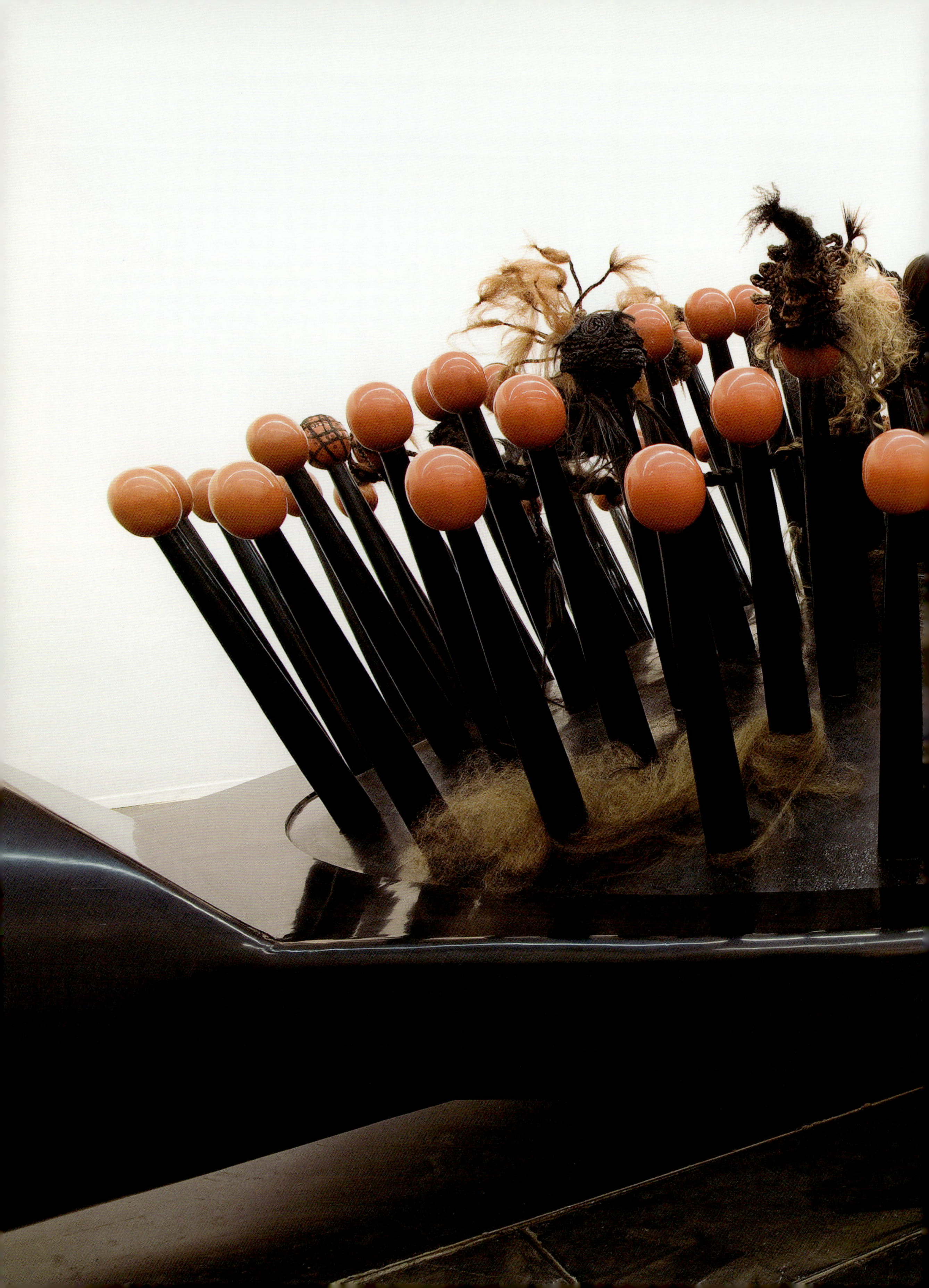

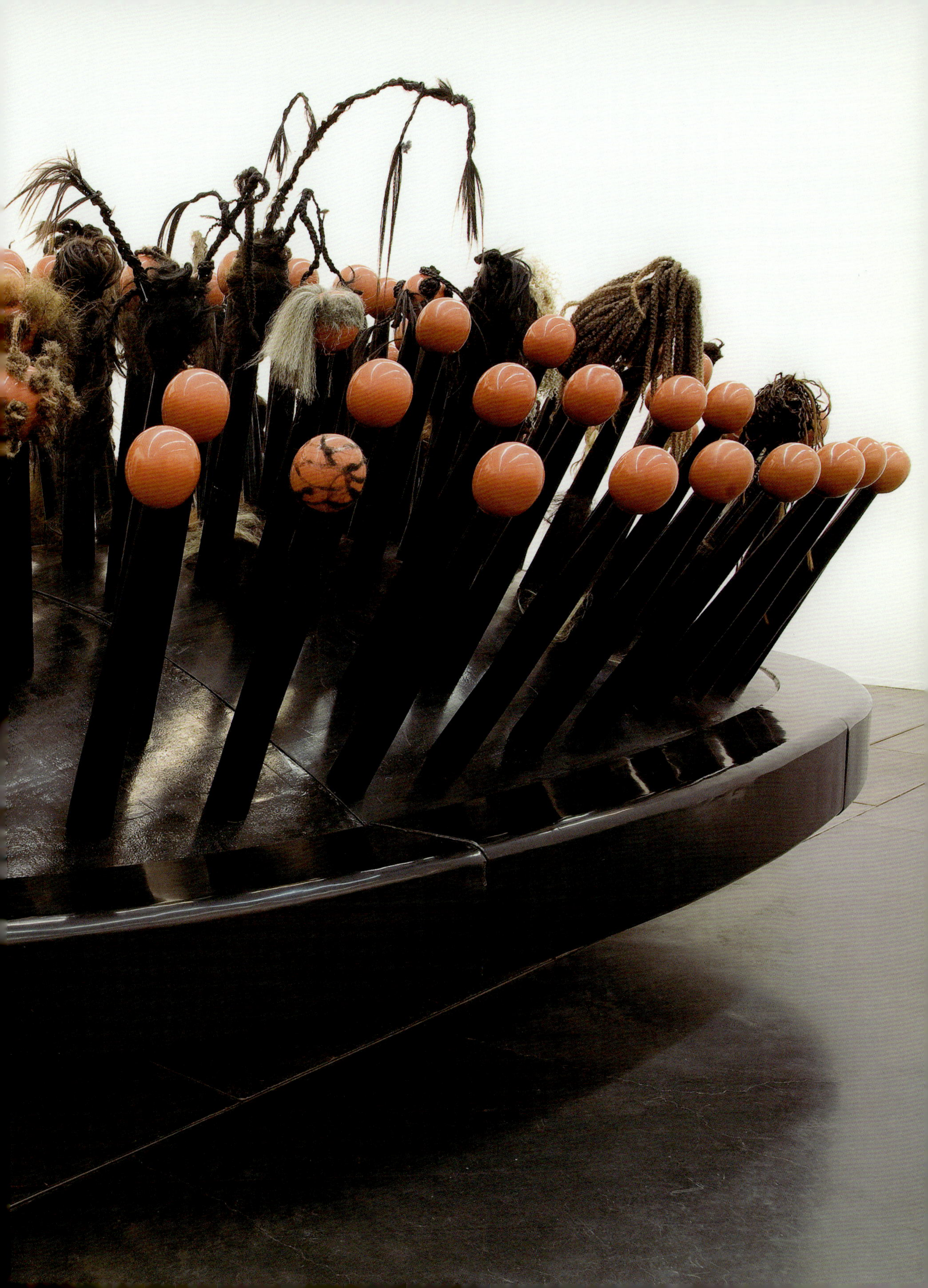

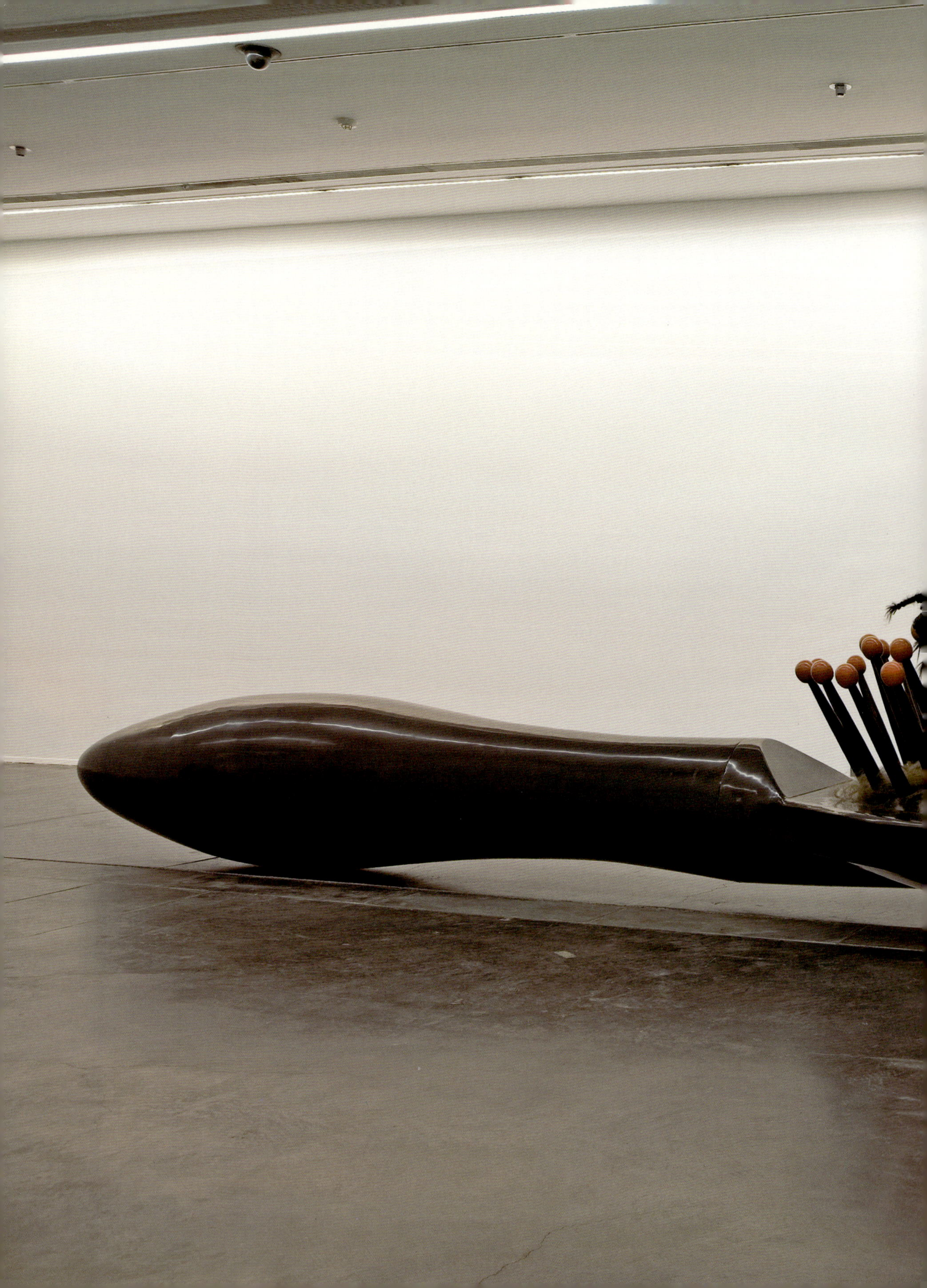

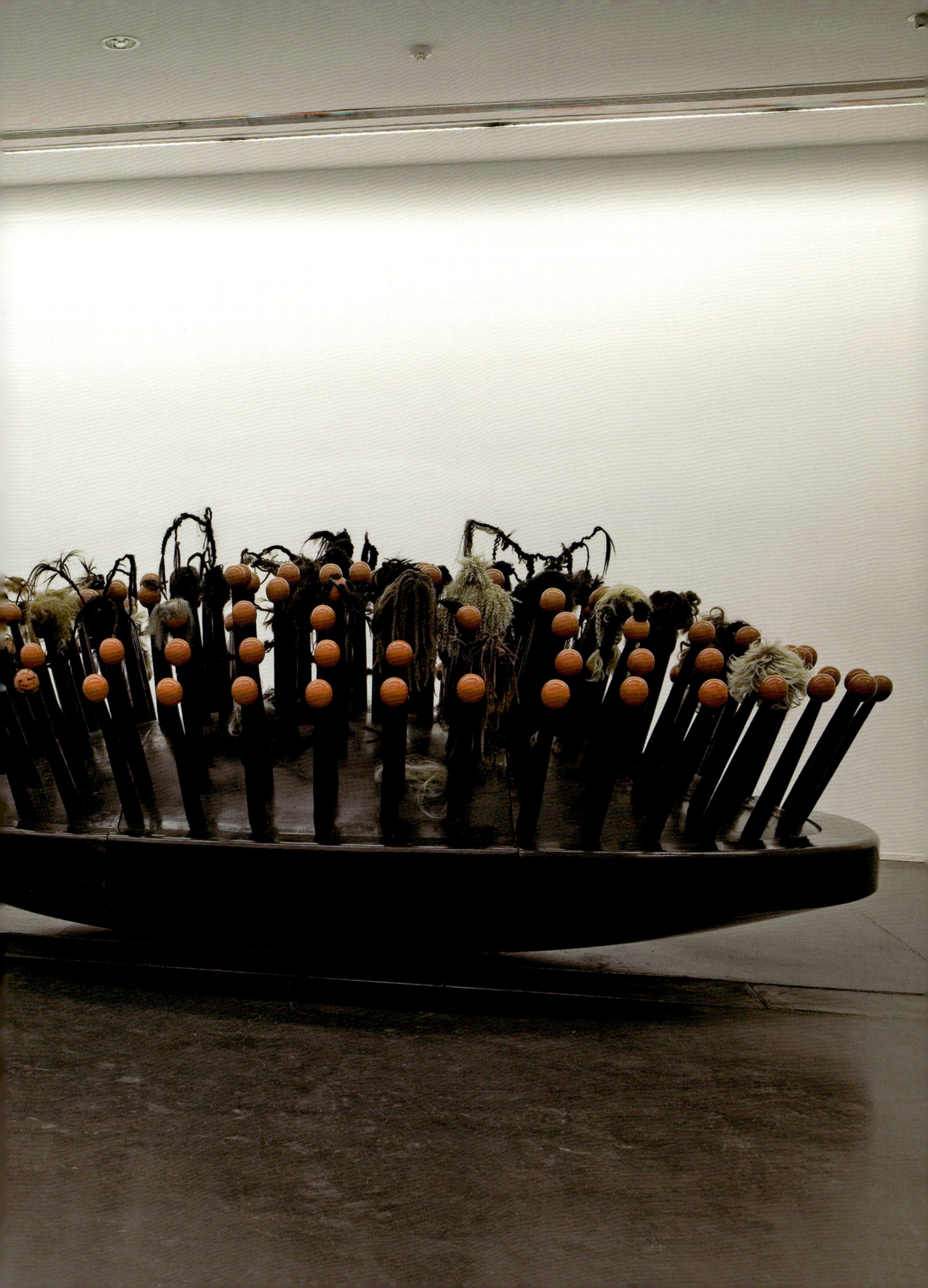

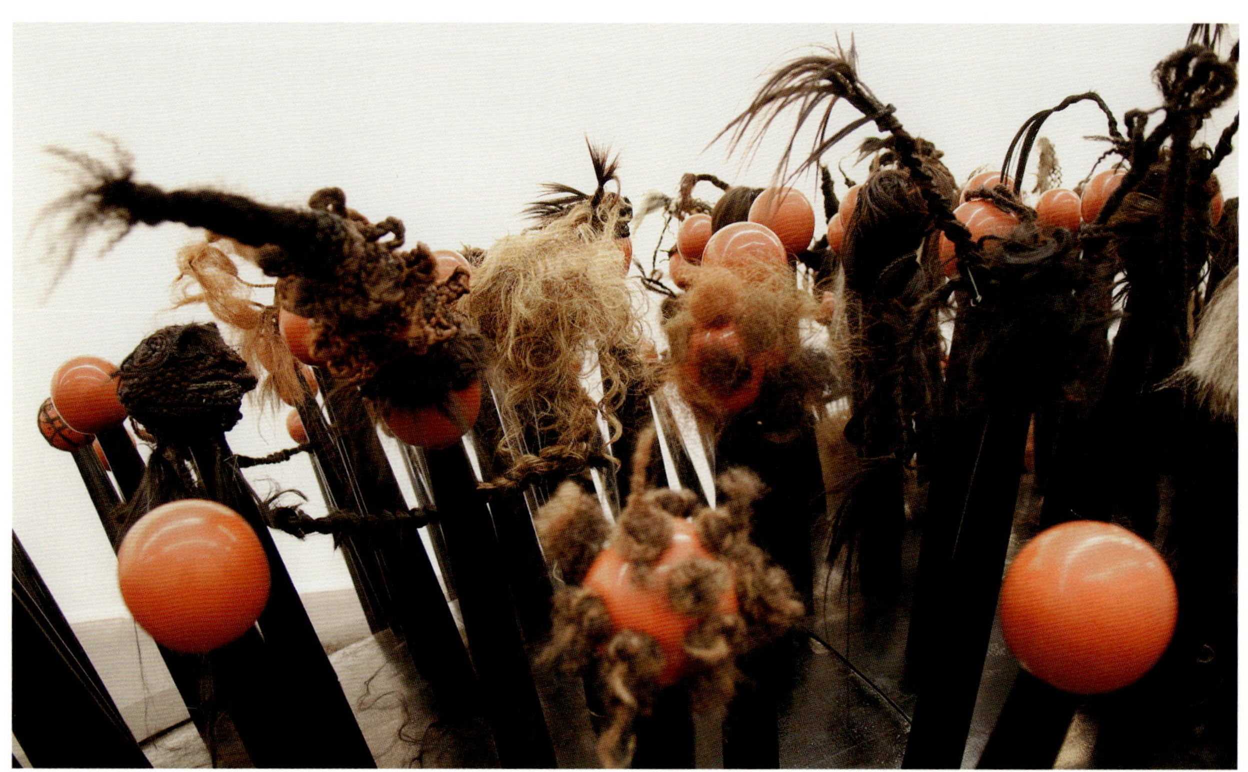

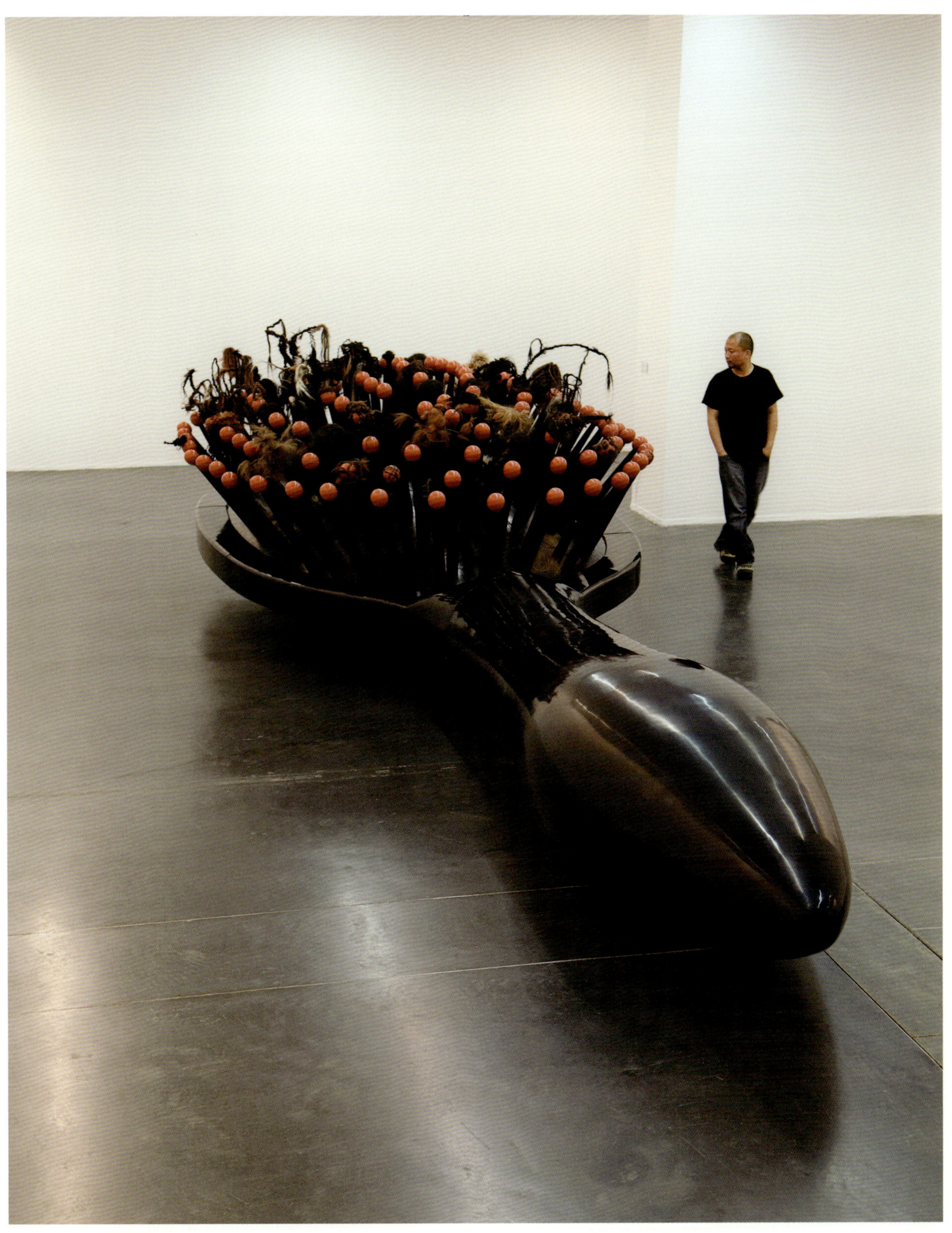

急促的话语
Hurried Words

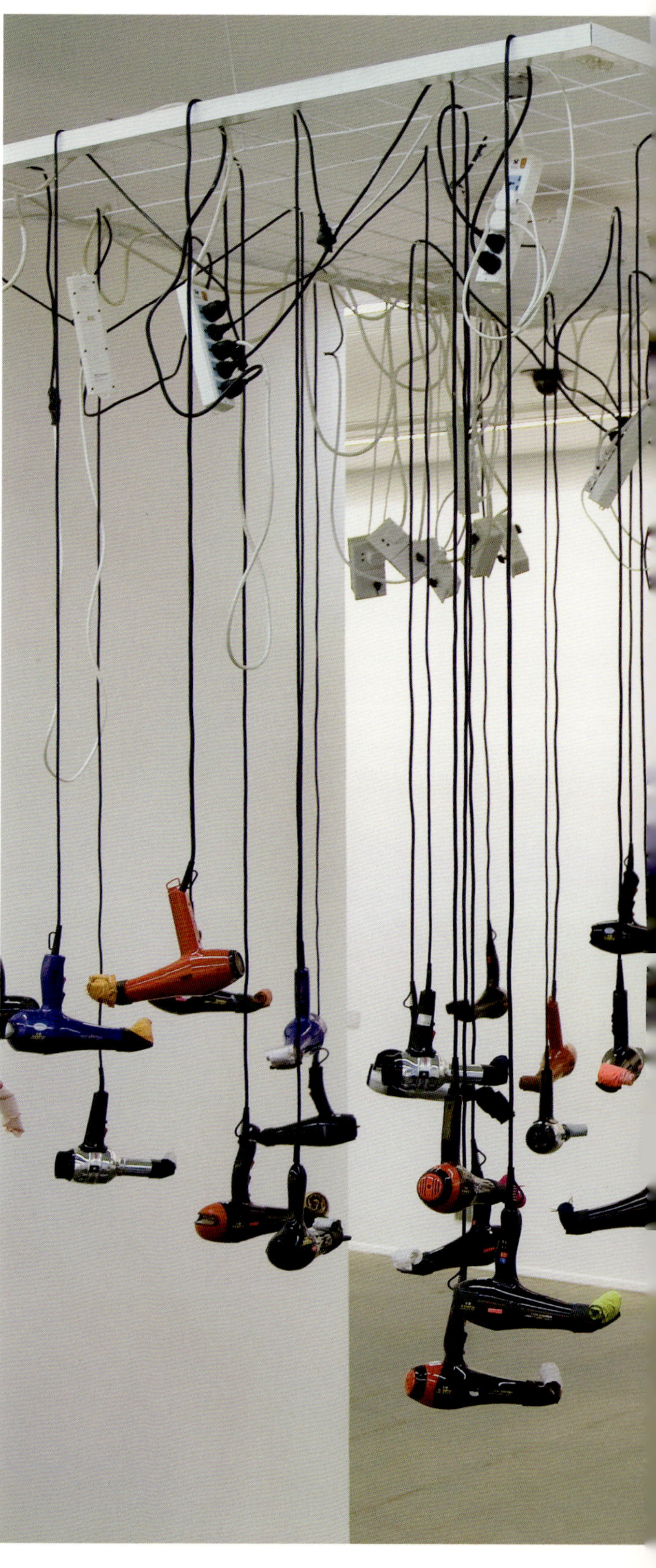

2008—2009年
装置
可变尺寸

2008 – 2009
Installation
Dimensions variable

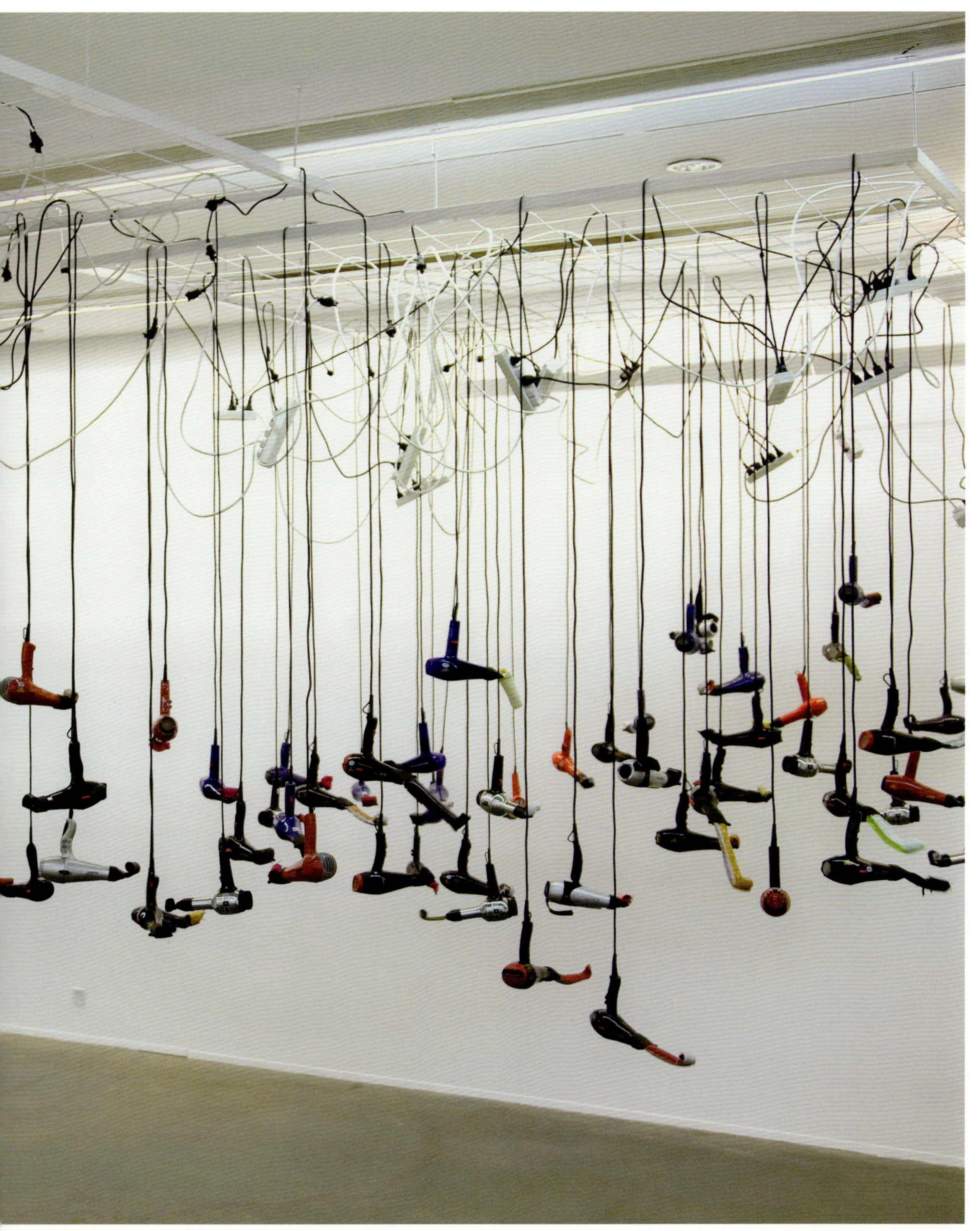

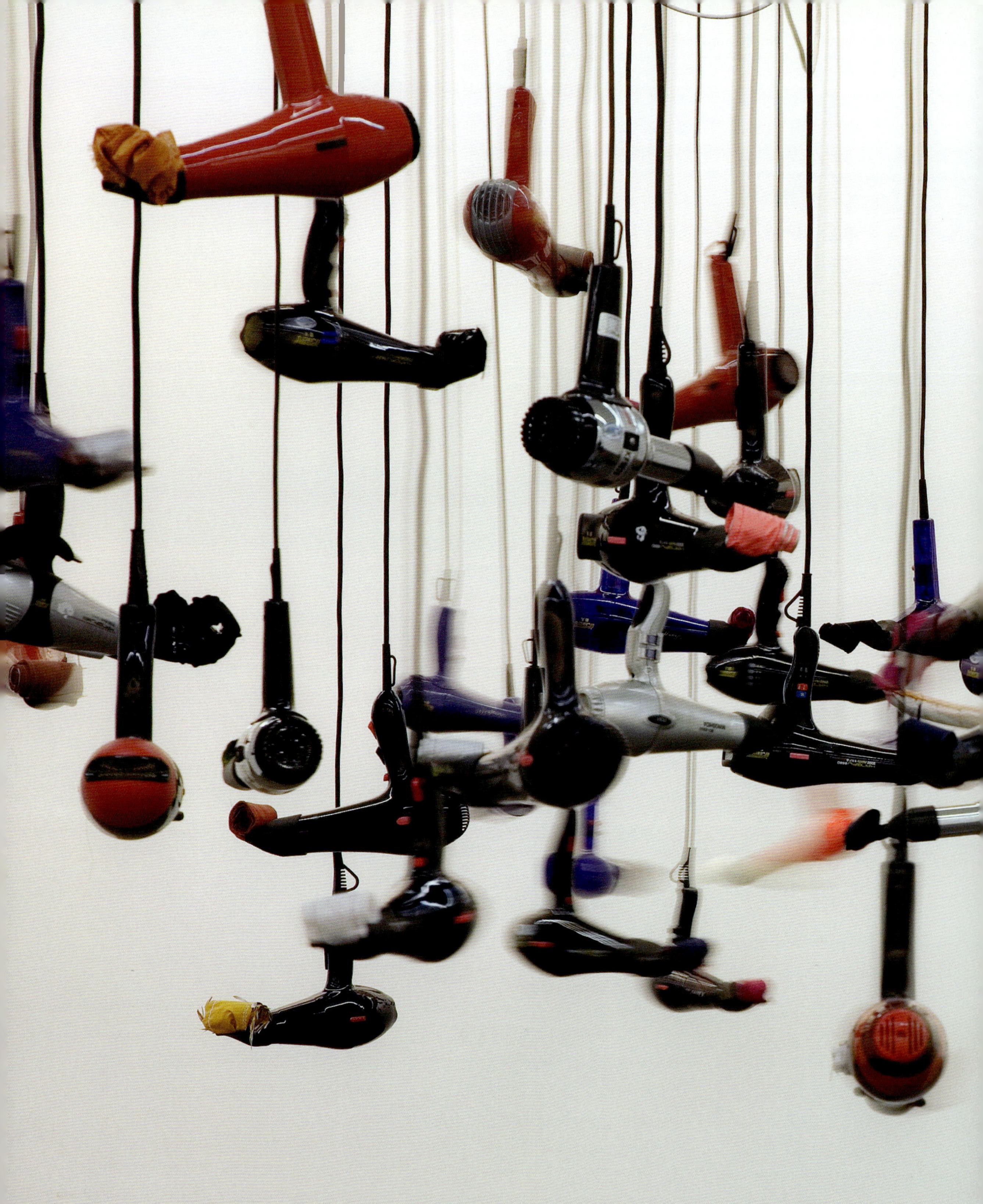

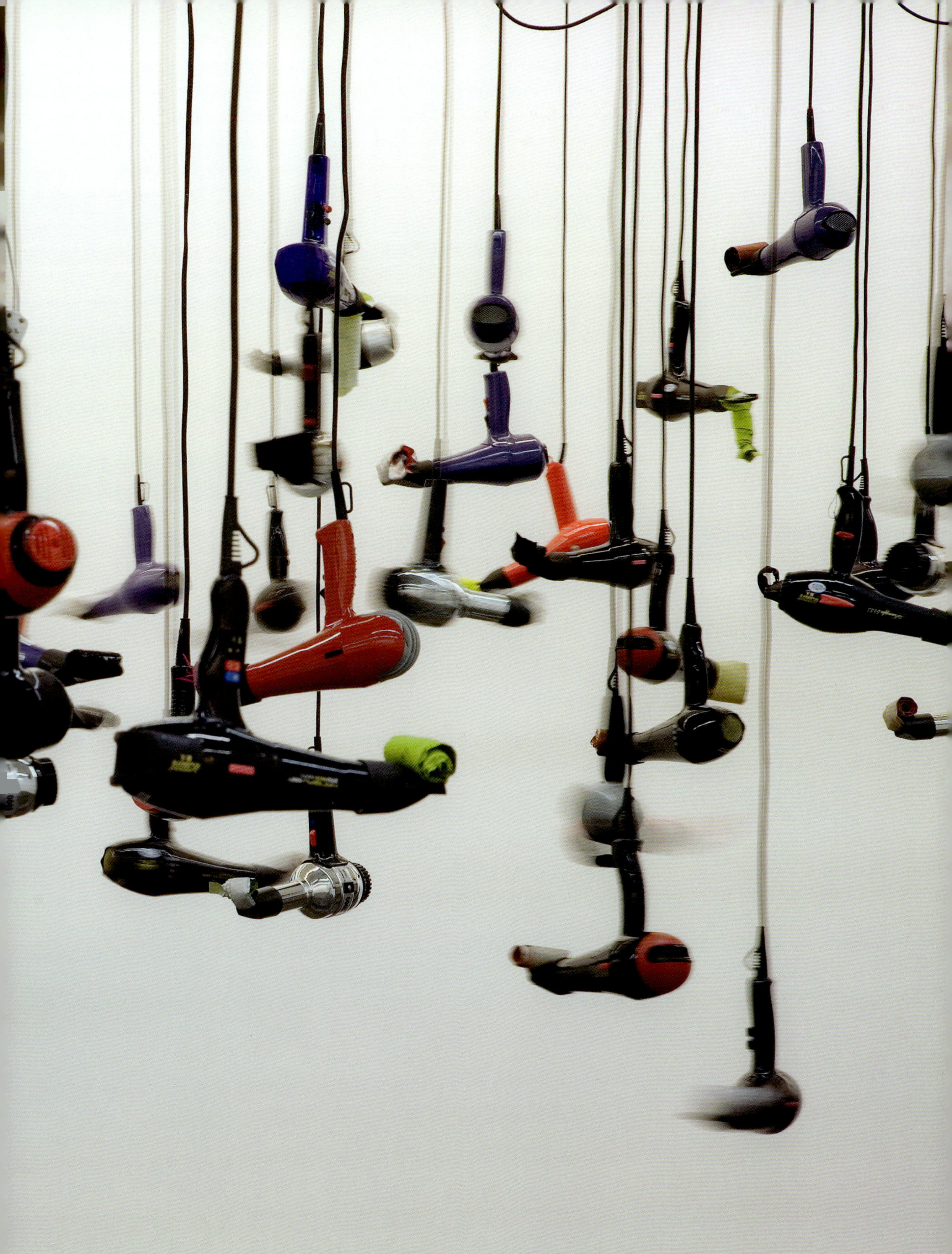

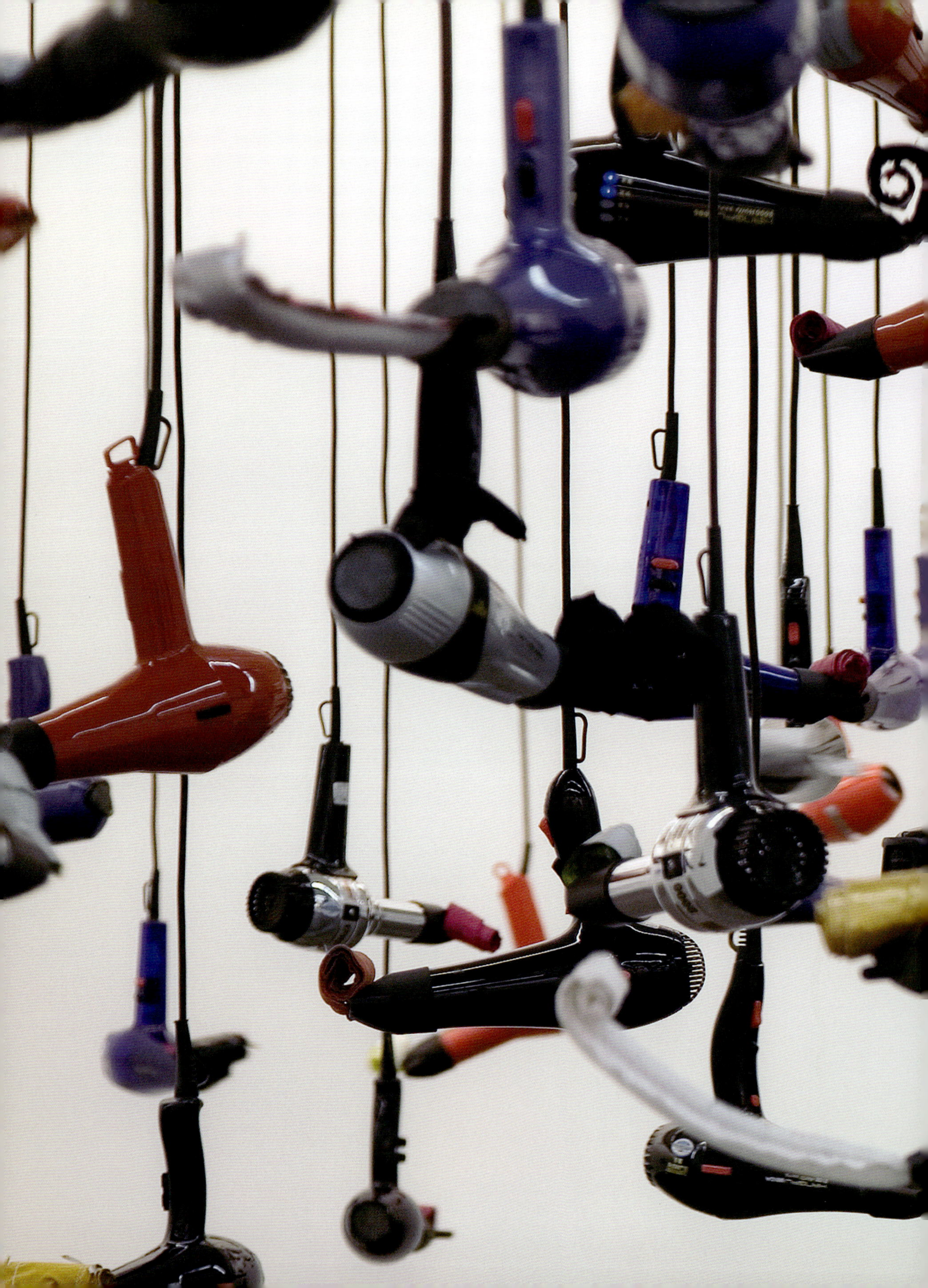

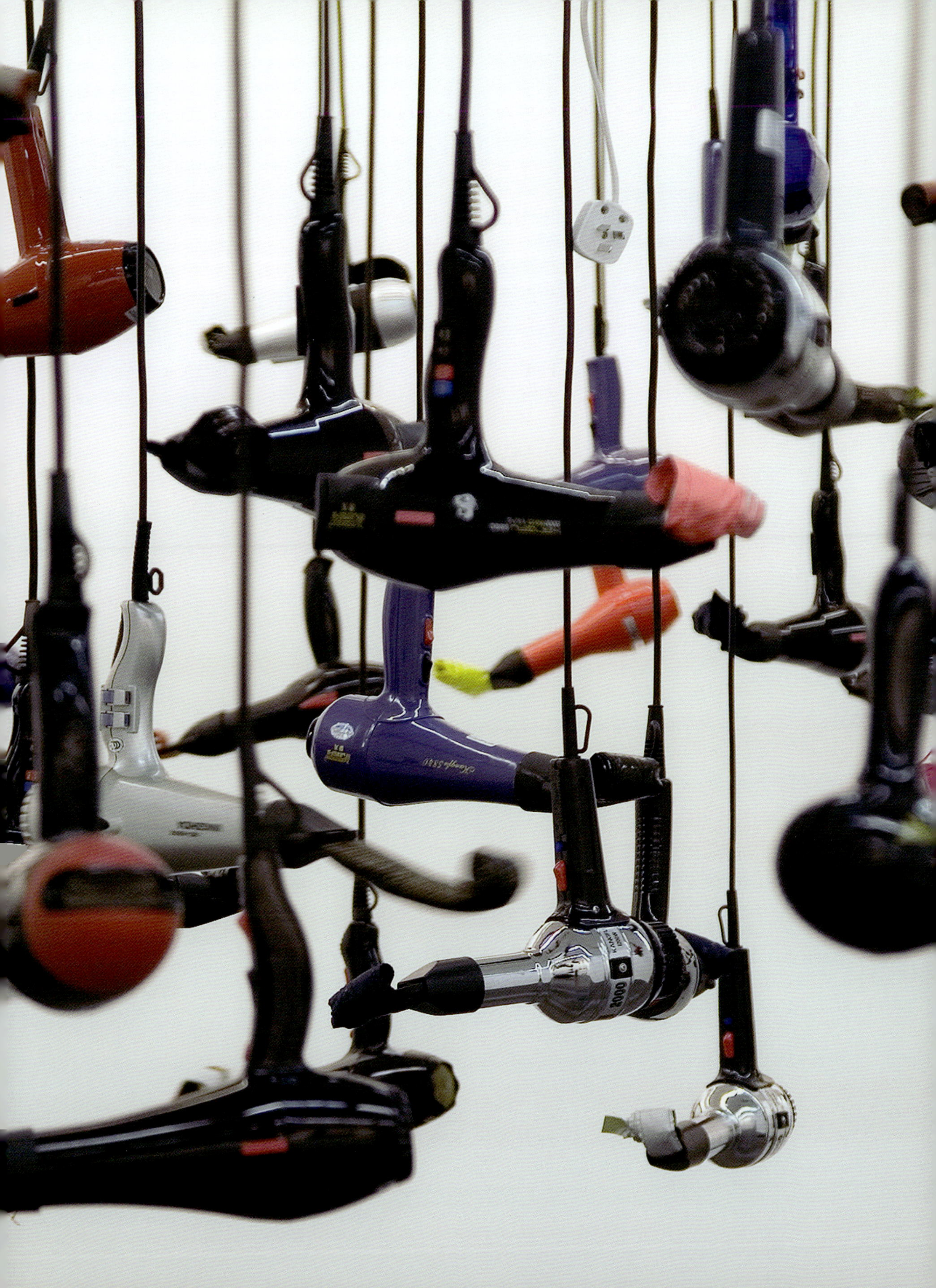

空间的零度
Le degré zero
de l'espace

2008年
录像
9分钟

2008
Video
9 minutes

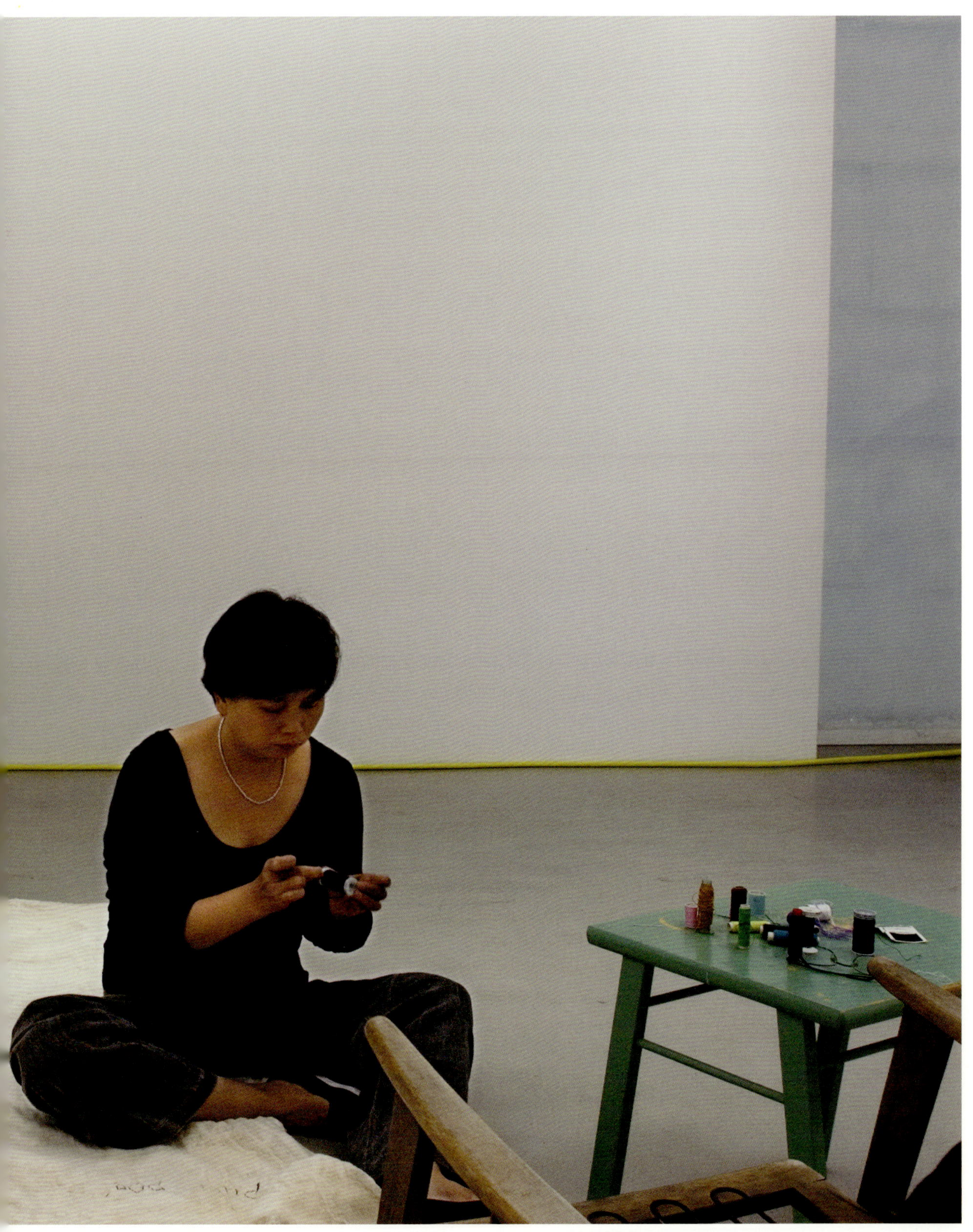

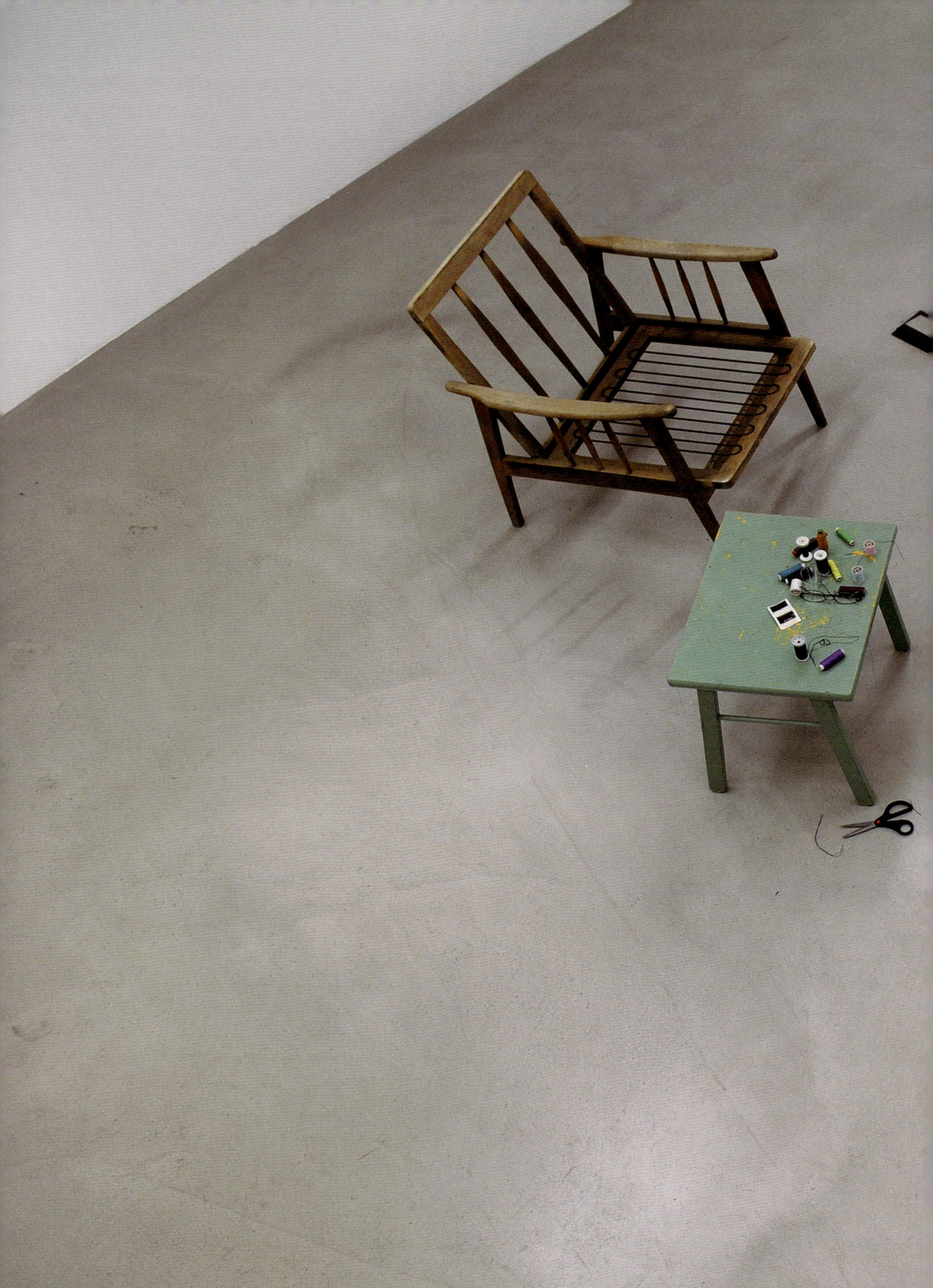

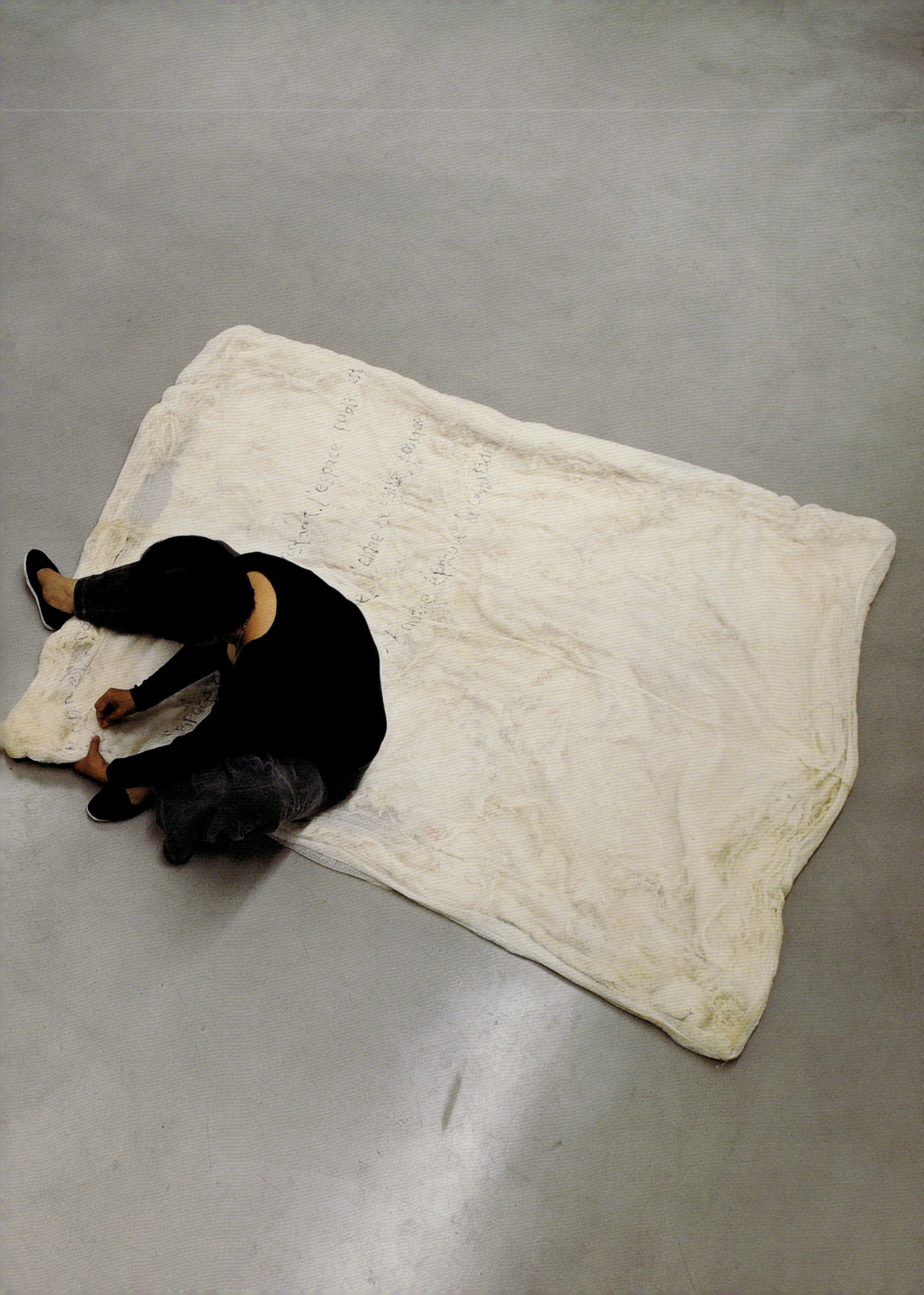

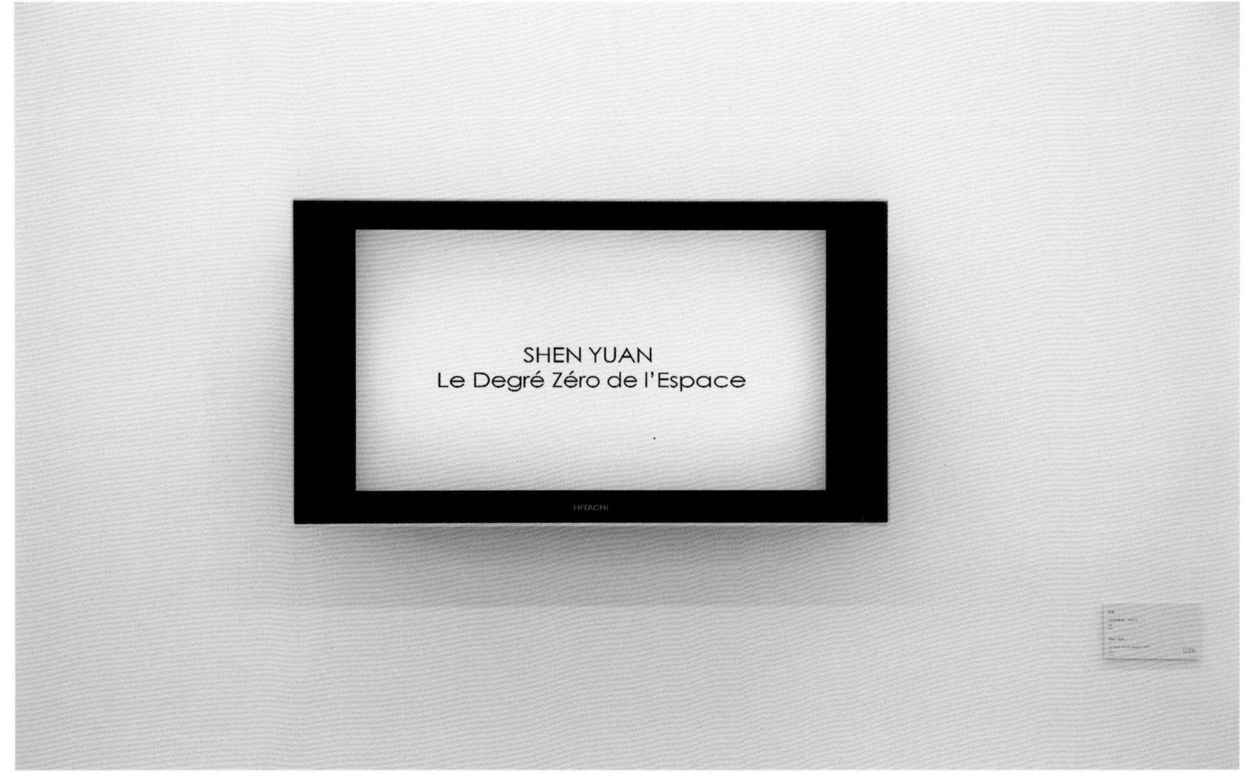
SHEN YUAN
Le Degré Zéro de l'Espace
HITACHI

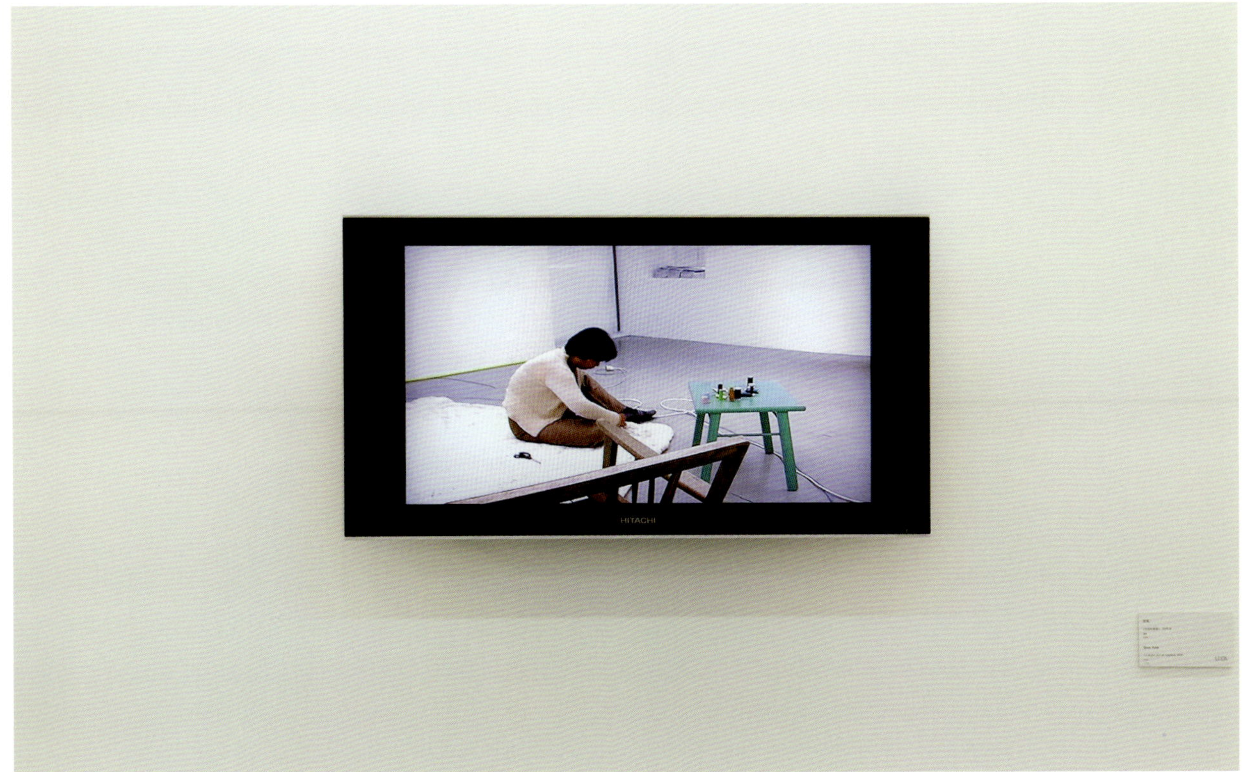

不舒适的鞋
她们离家出走，却无处可去

Uncomfortable Shoes
(*Elles sont parties, pourtant elles n'ont nulle part où aller*)

2008年
装置
可变尺寸

2008
Installation
Dimensions variable

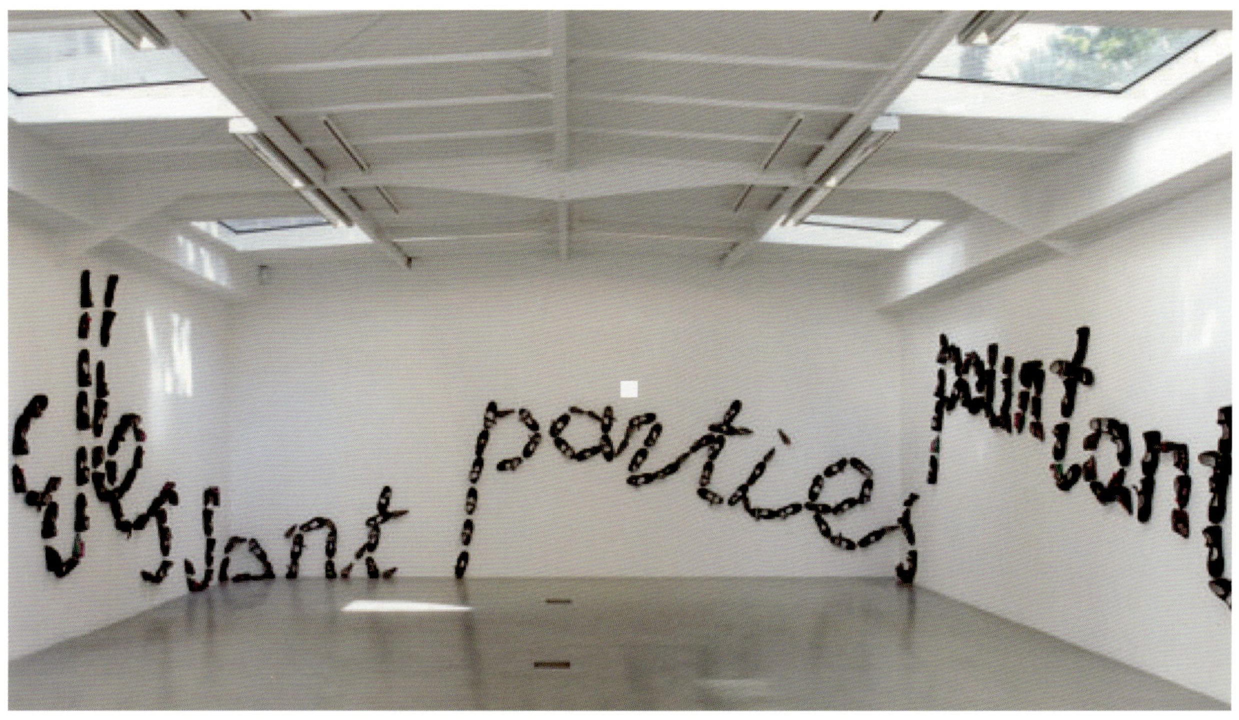

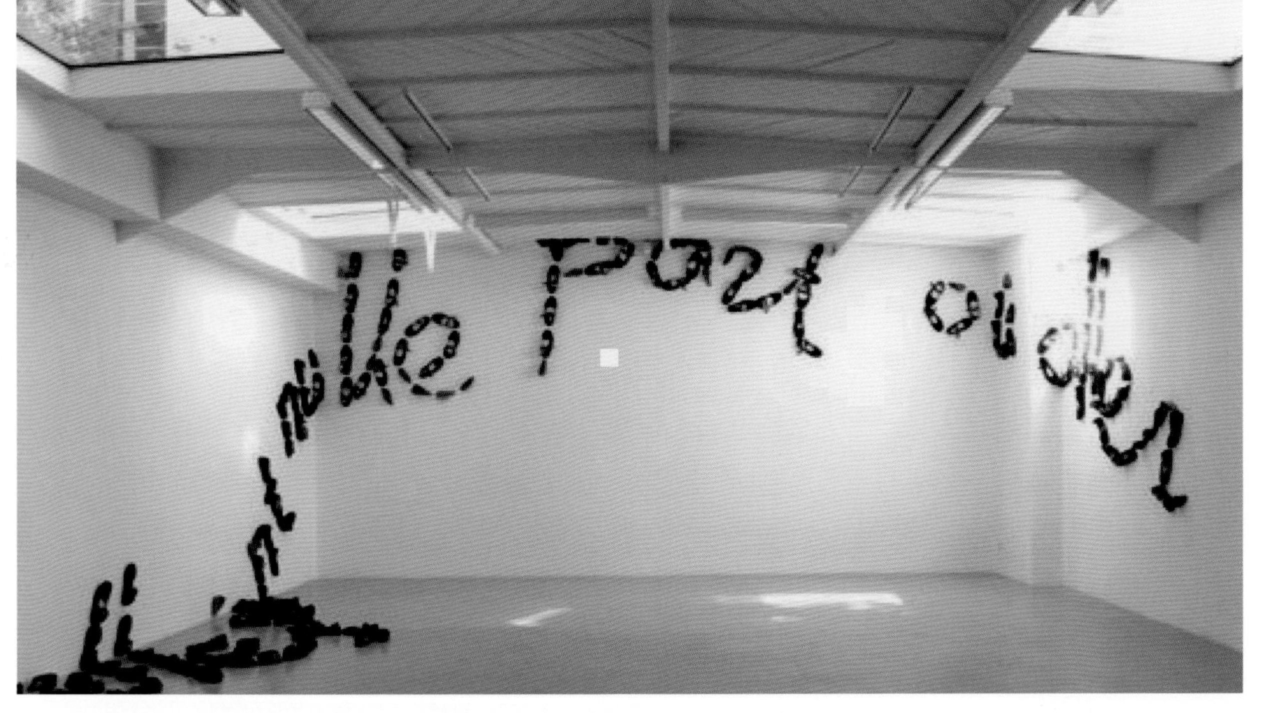

仙游
Errance immortelle

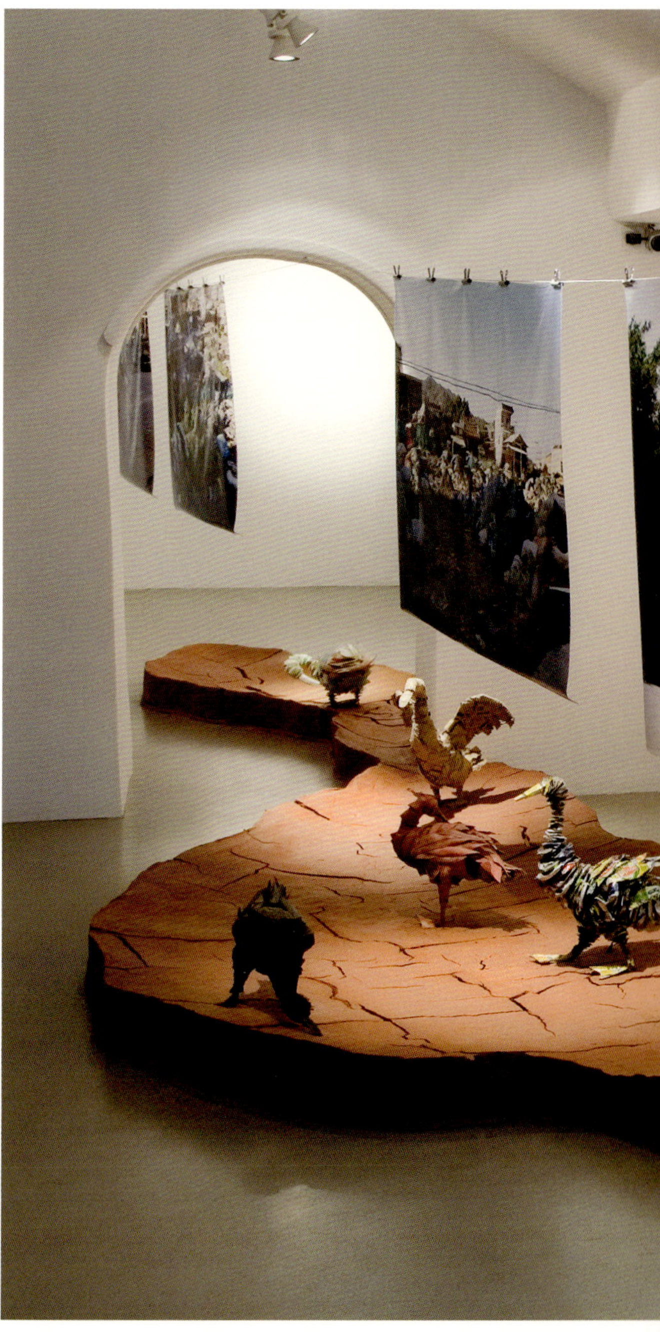

2008年
装置
200×700×200 厘米

2008
Installation
200×700×200 cm

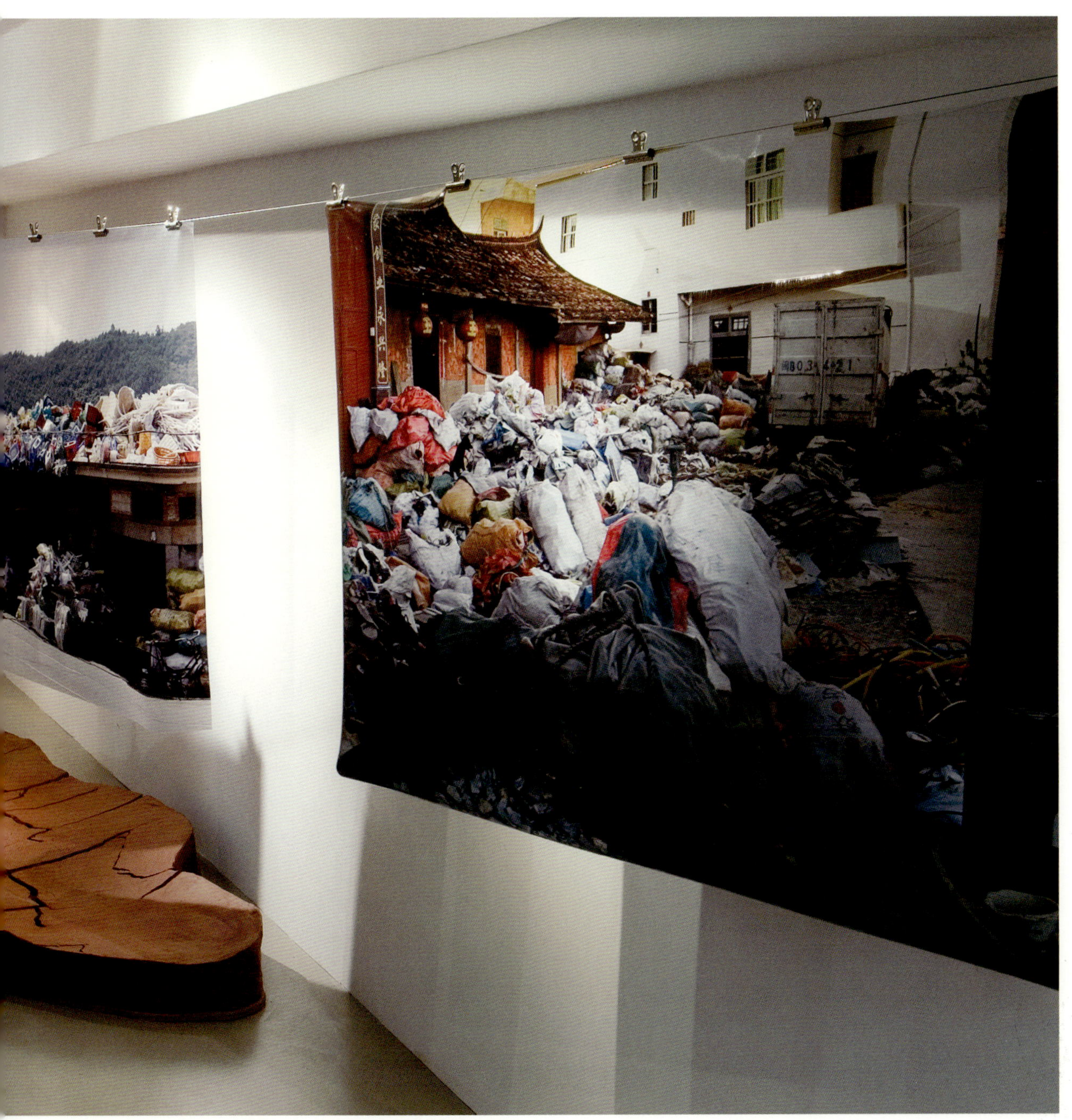

变温动物
Poïkilotherme

2008年
装置
302×18×22 厘米

2008
Installation
302×18×22 cm

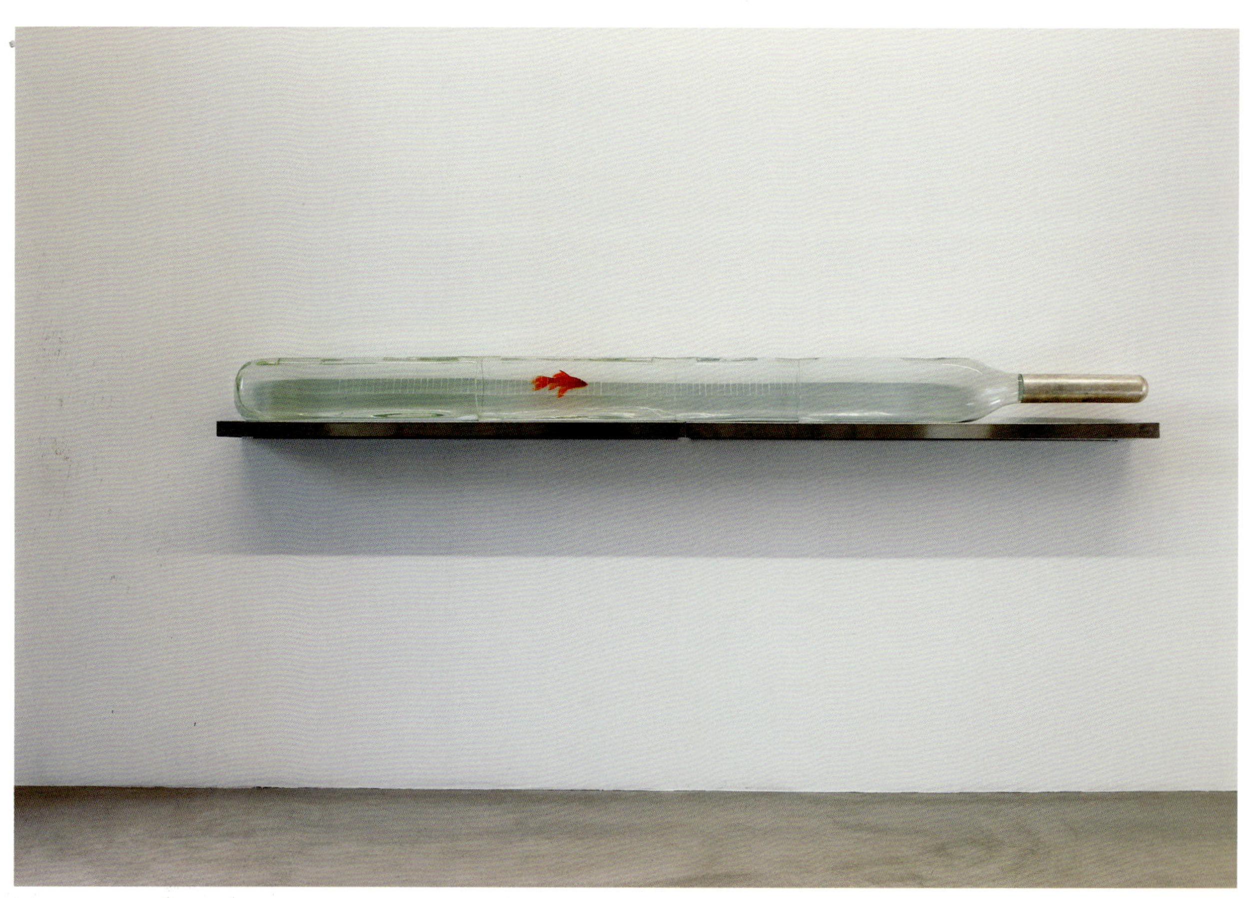

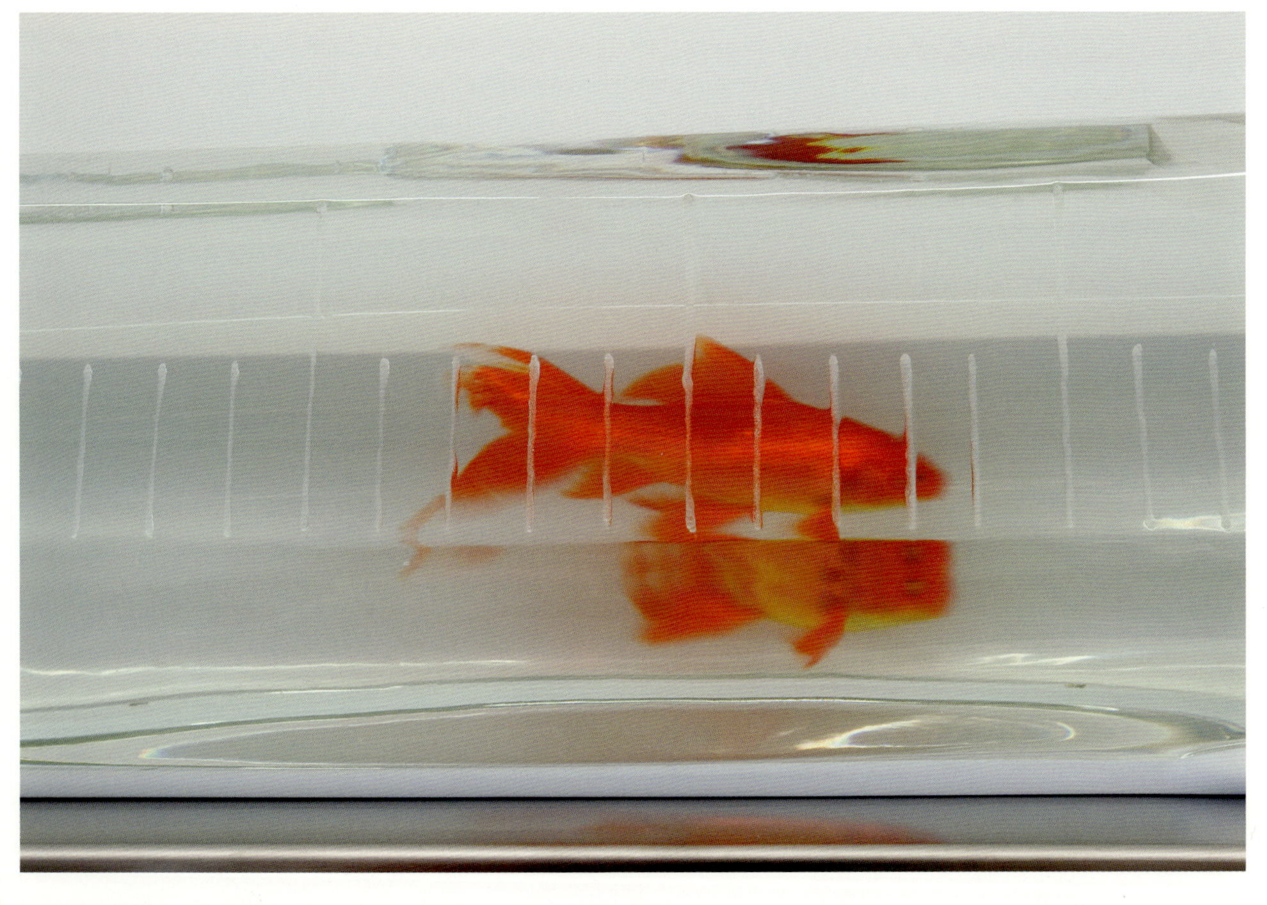

石腹

Le ventre de pierre

2008年
装置
200×165×60厘米

2008
Installation
200×165×60 cm

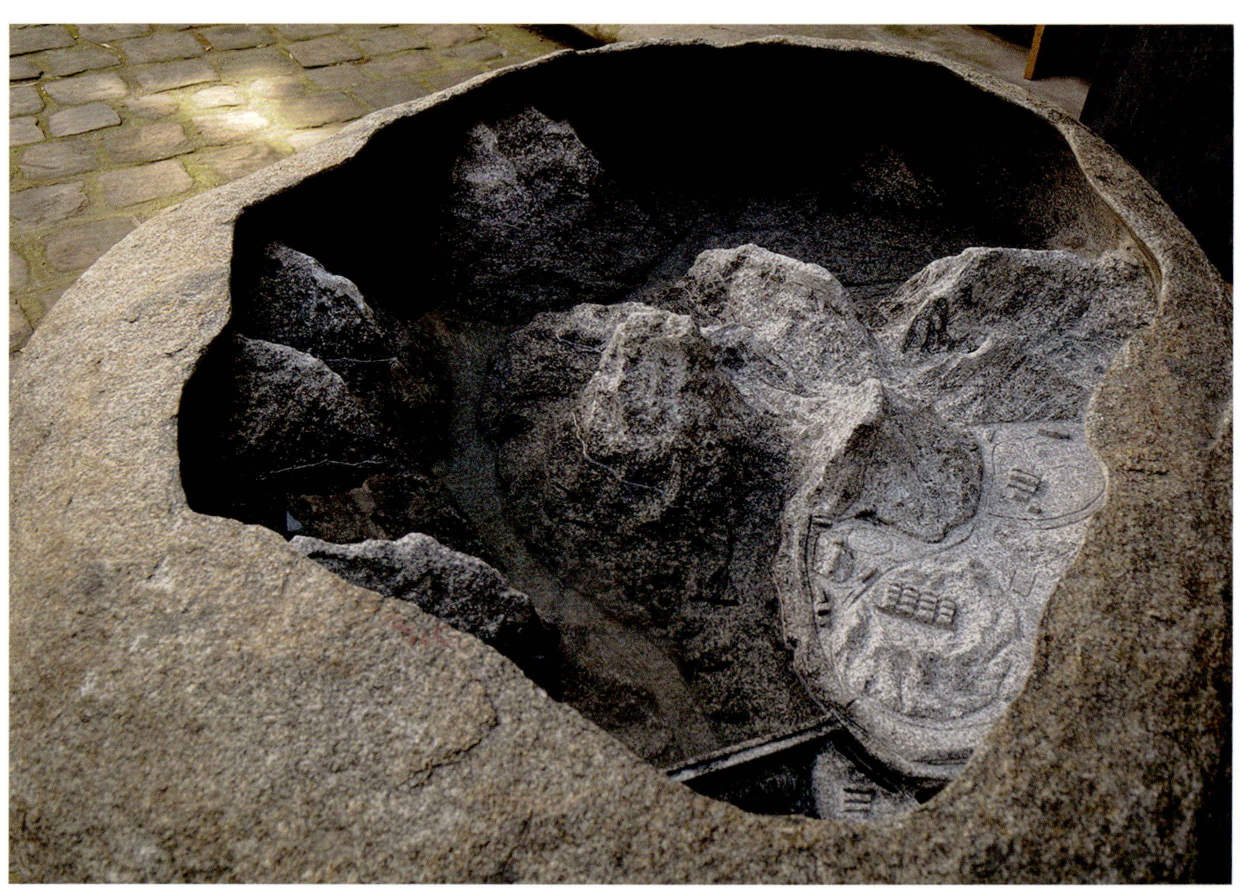

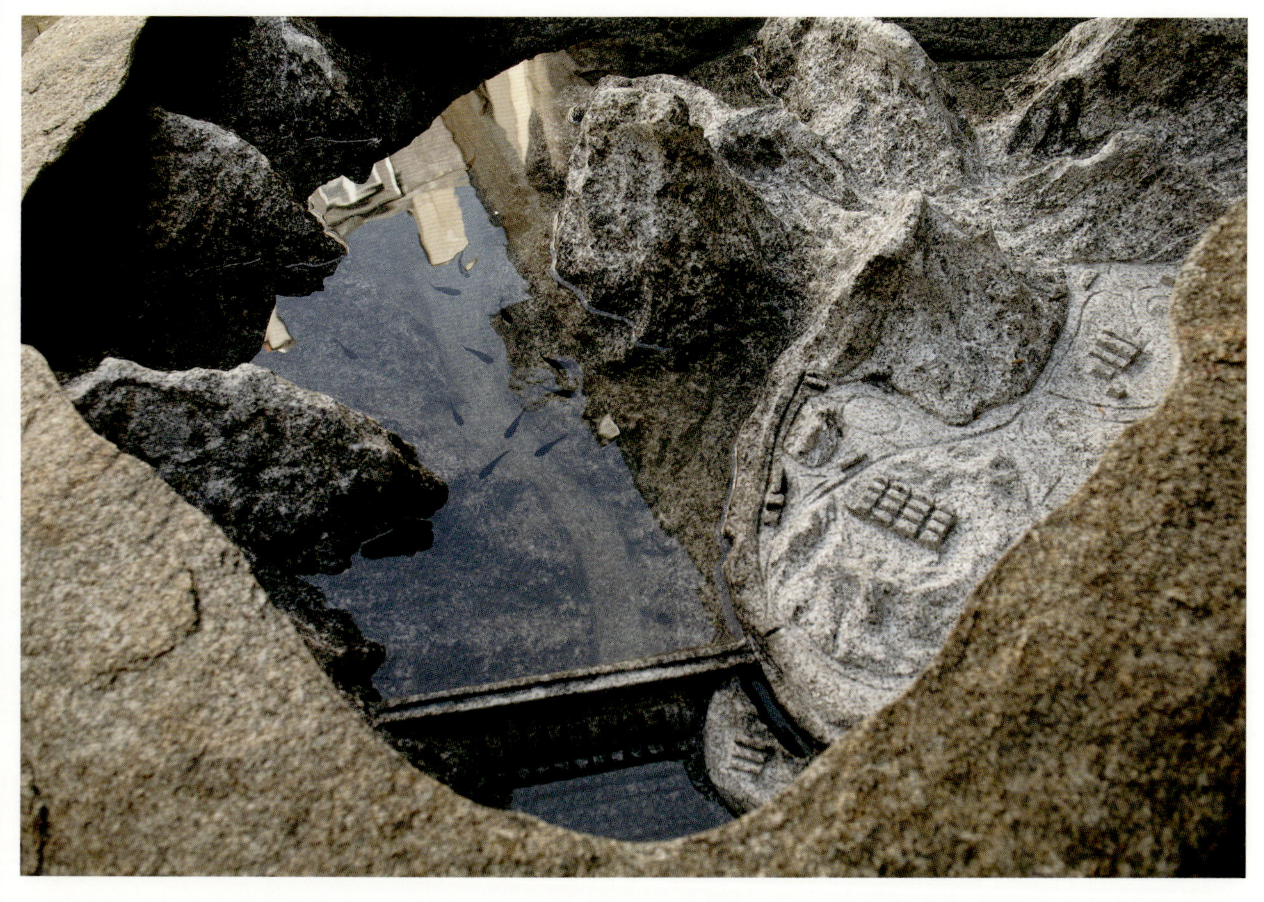

初次旅行
First Trip

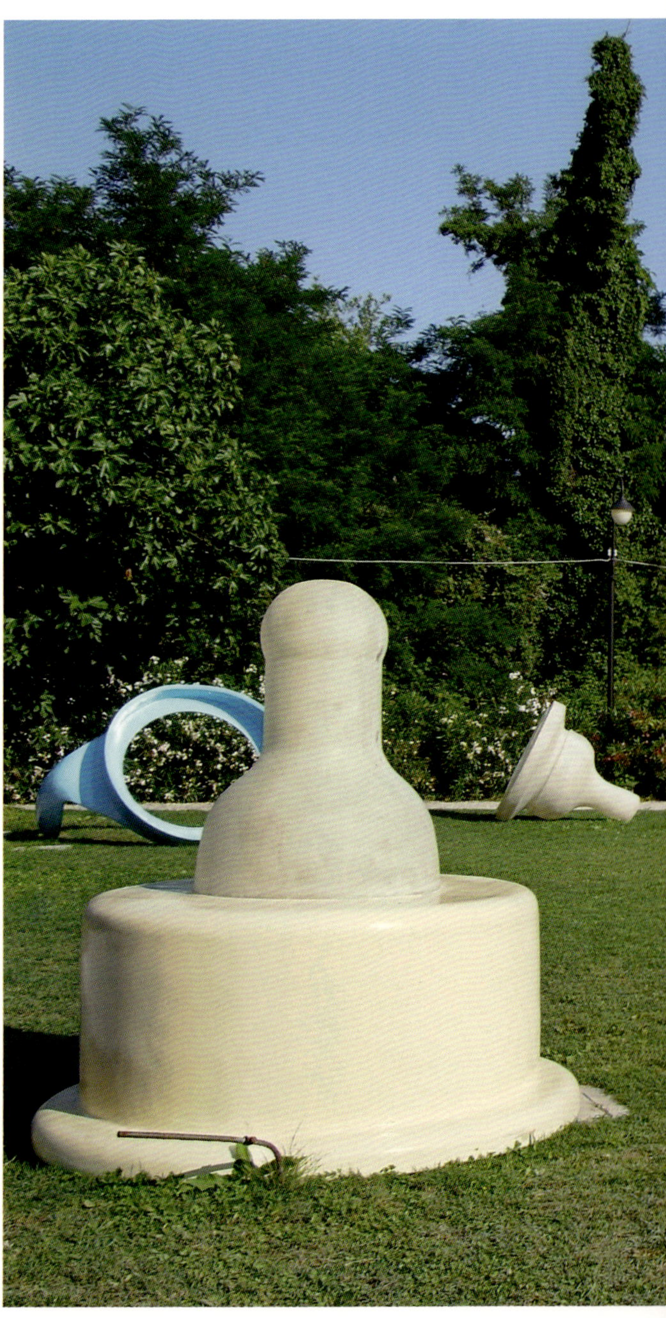

2007年
装置
1200×1200×250厘米

2007
Installation
1200×1200×250 cm

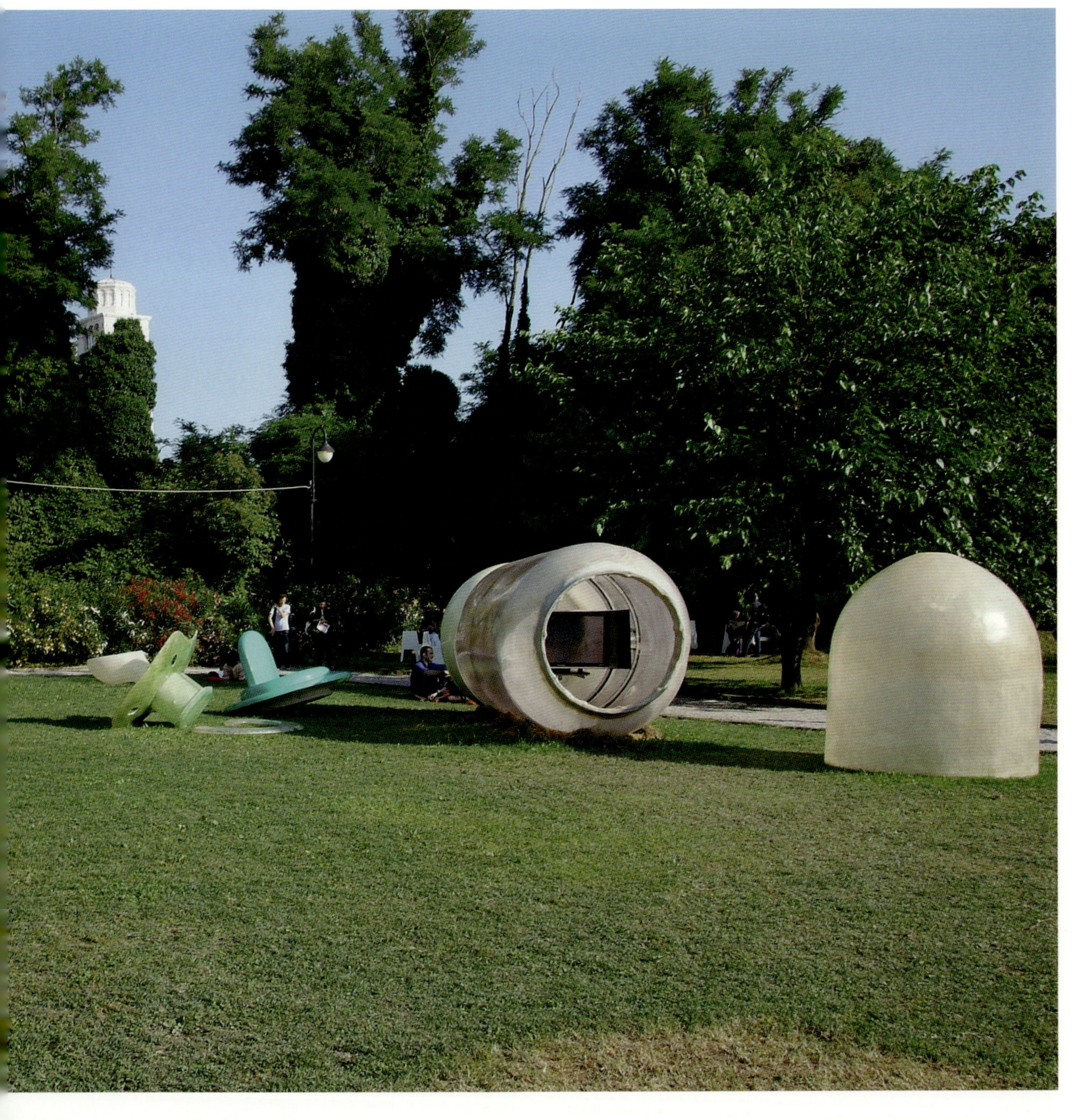

恐龙蛋

The Dinosaur Egg:
A Kinder Surprise

2001—2006年
装置
1000×1200×120厘米

2001 – 2006
Installation
1000×1200×120 cm

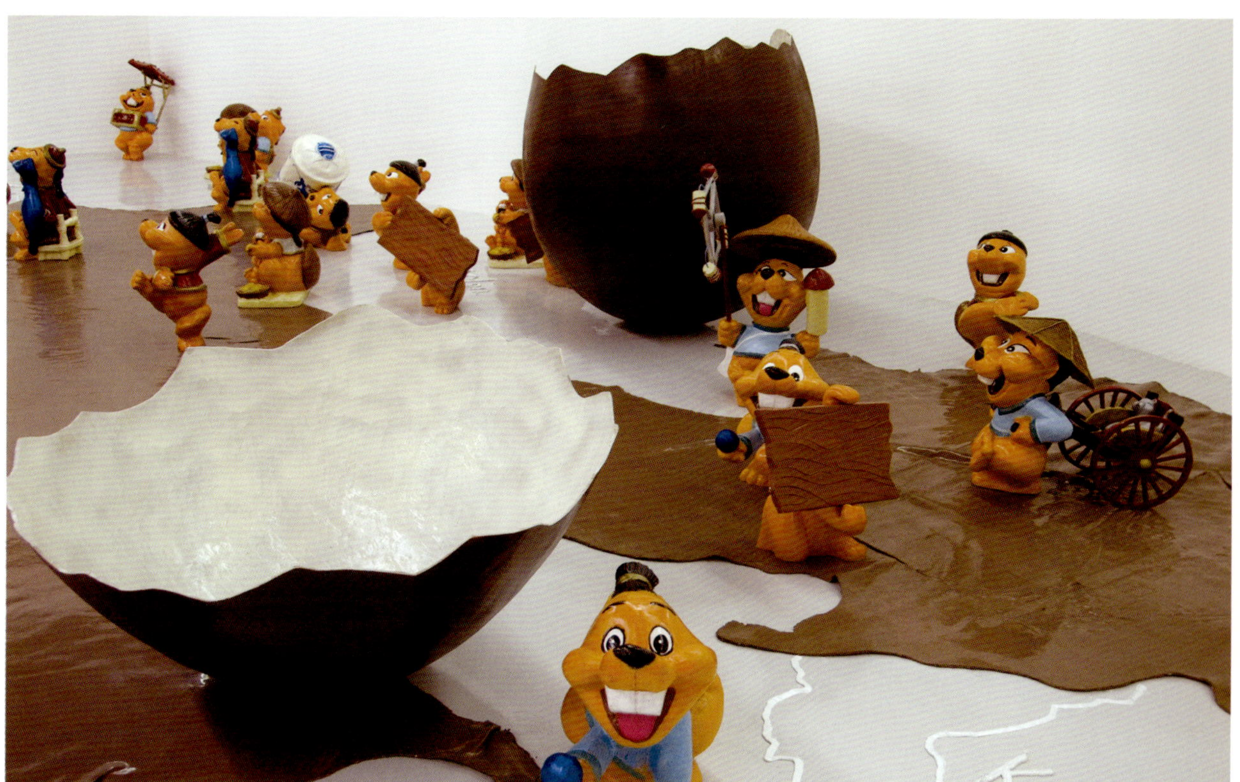

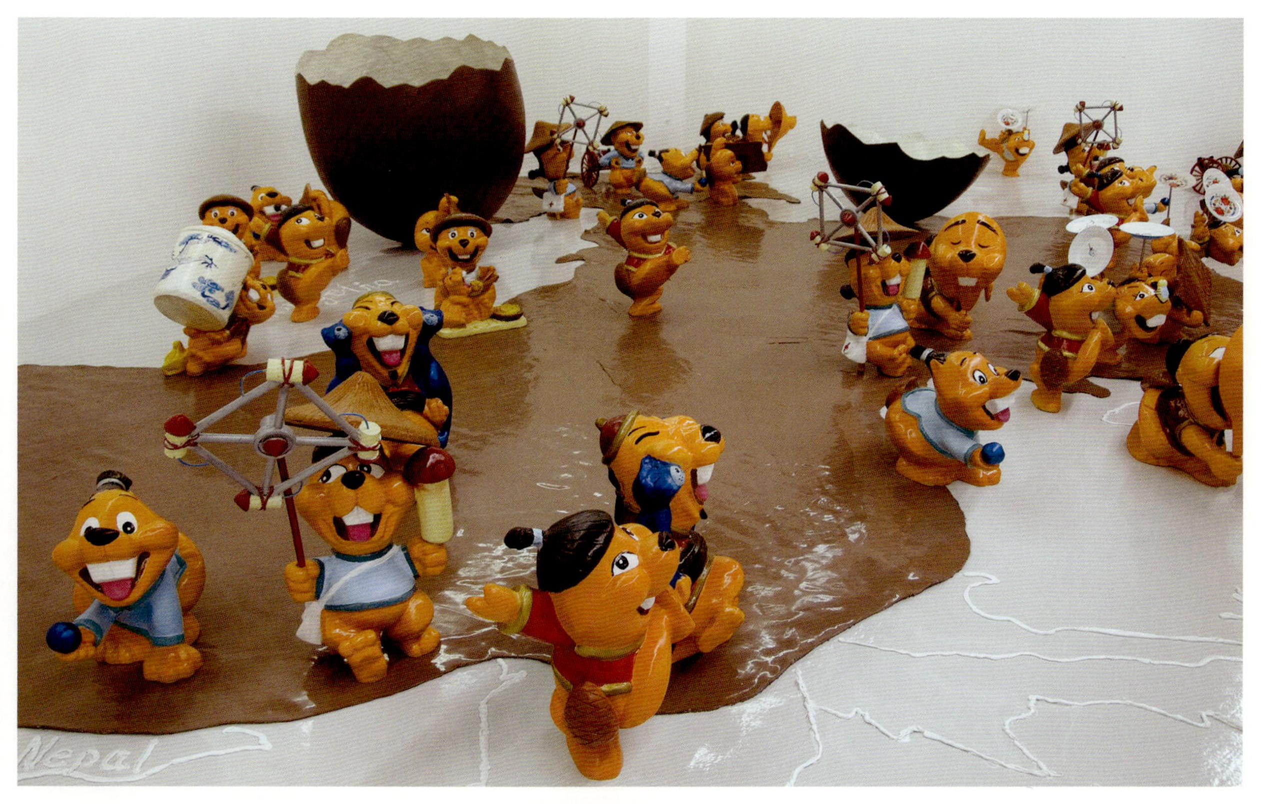

南岭史
（南岭妇女书写）

History of Nanling
(*Written by Women from Nan Mountains*)

2005年
装置
1000×900×150厘米

2005
Installation
1000×900×150 cm

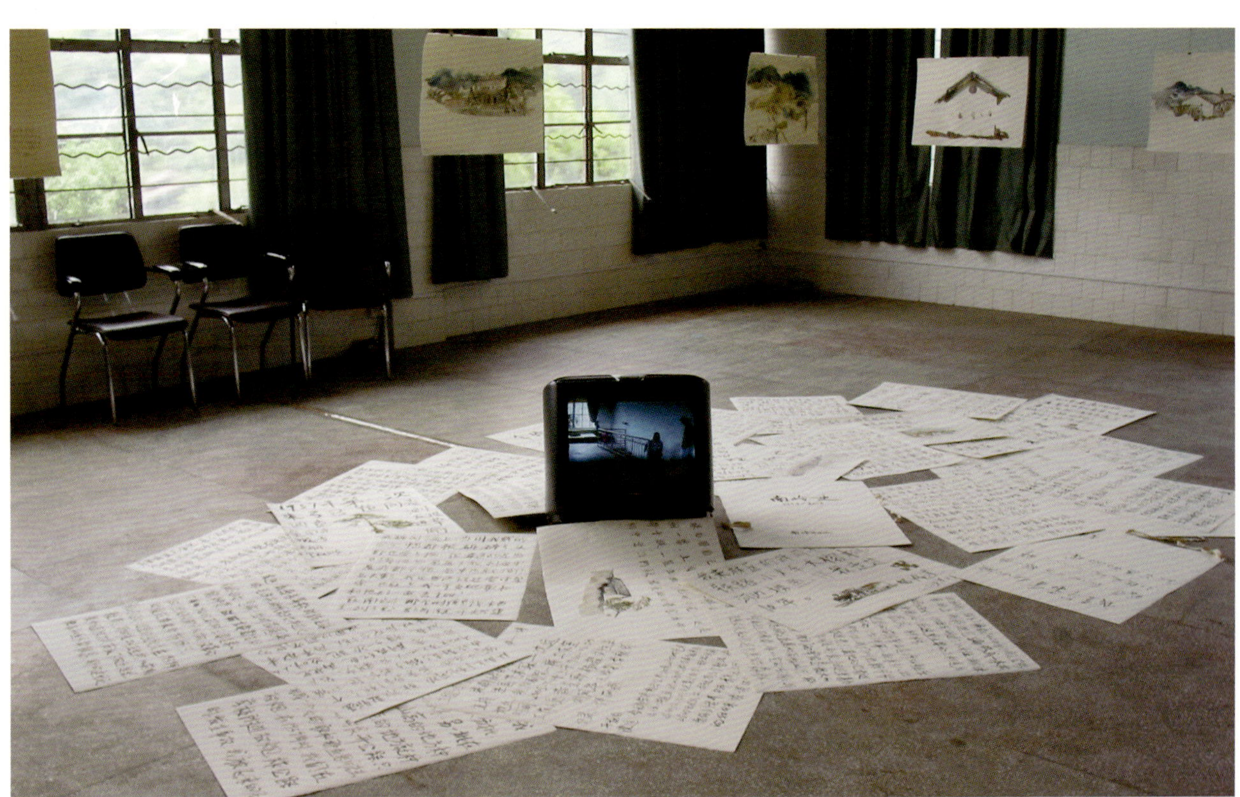

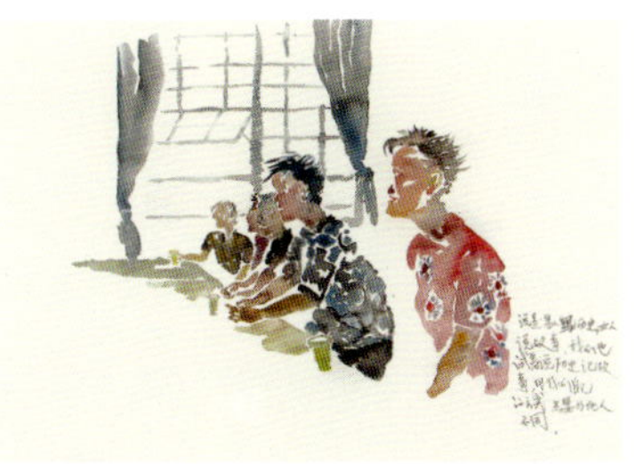 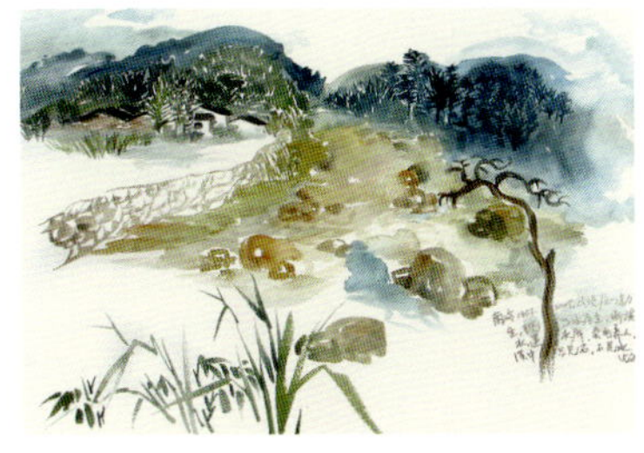 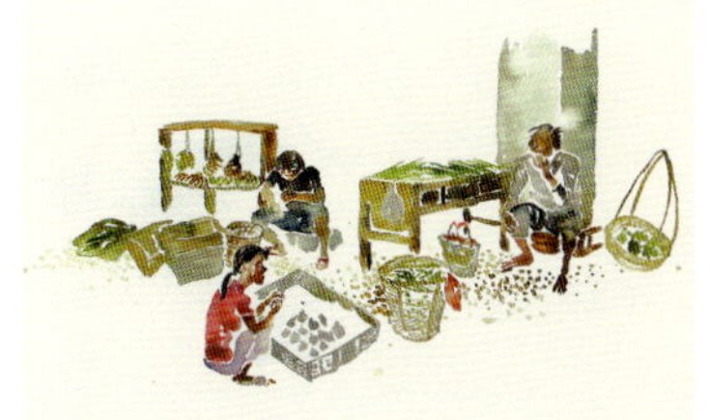

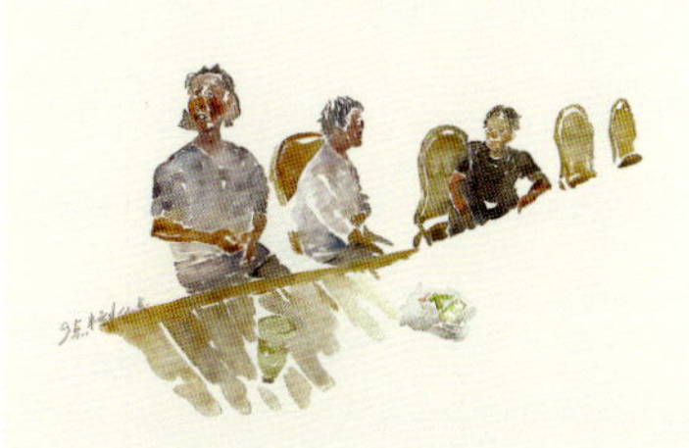 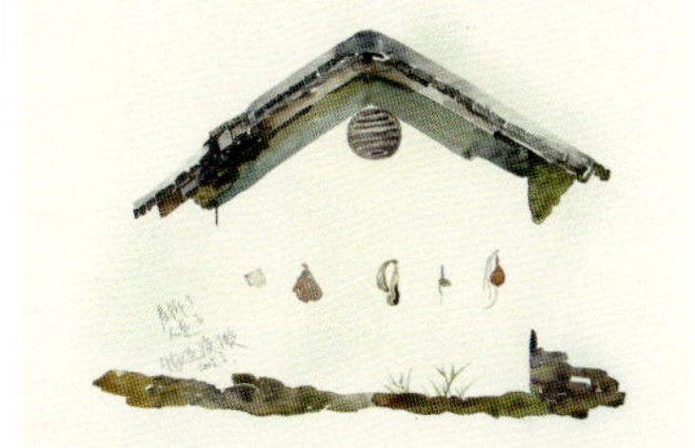 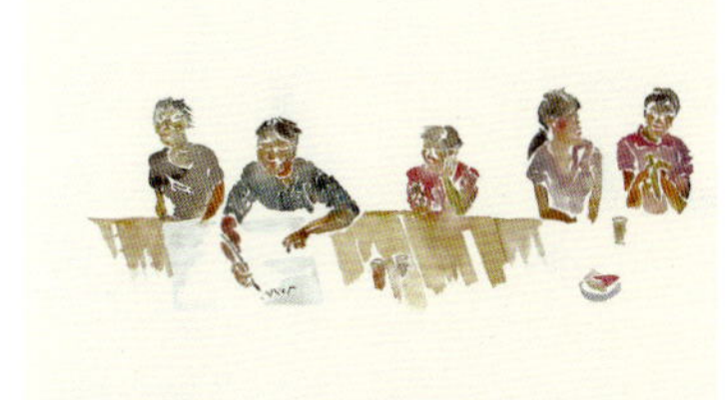

主题：南岭妇女艺术活动——讲述南岭的历史
主持：法国艺术家—沈远
地点：乳阳剧院二楼工作室
时间：2005-7-14上午 9:30—11:00
工作人员：黄星海、杨超、刘主任
刘凤华、王玲南、李银妹
记录：许丽燕

开场白
沈远：今天非常感谢各位参加南岭的妇女艺术活动，讲述南岭的历史。很有幸能来南岭创作。当听说这里还没有一部书写南岭的历史的书，我就有了个想法，邀请你们老年、中年、青年三个年龄段的妇女来谈谈你们对南岭的回忆。你们将自己的回忆用毛笔写在纸上，我将把它编写成一本书。

南岭妇女：1958年，刚过了八月节，我们就到南岭。在这里主要的工种是后勤、盖房、种树。

南岭妇女：这里的前身单位是1956年在乐昌开始的。1957年第一批来了八位同志，其中有一位，我们叫他赖爷爷的，去年91岁过老了，其他的也都过老了。这八位同志到乳阳这里勘察、测量。我们的单位是很大的，以前是国家直属的省林业厅。那时由于工作需要，服从党的安排随丈夫来到了这个原始森林。

草长得很高很宽，甚至还有刺。那个时候我们的孩子还很小，我们都是用箩筐挑着从很远的山脚城走过来。

南岭妇女：省府本来想在这里搞一个10万人口以上的林业城。由于水源问题（水源不足）最后没有建成。后来59年来了第二批移民到这里，但到了石年代末80年代初，人员逐渐减少（到深圳、珠海打工）。93年筹划，94年南岭国家森林公园开始对外开

水把小火车铁路冲垮了。我们那时的第六大队分批，一批在山上砍木，另一批在山上种树。山高的地方种松树，低一点的地方就种上杉树。那时候开公路，只有我一个女的敢和那些男同志放炮，在1959年时，我们在学校附近放炮炸公路时发生事故，我被飞来的石

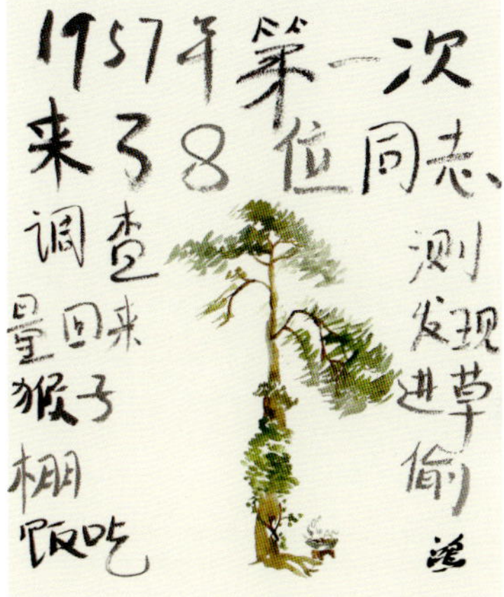

从山上下到河边，就掀起锅盖偷吃东西。后来我们想了一个办法赶走了猴子，我们把一只猴子的头顶上的头发剃光。之后用油漆刷成红色，再把它放走。猴子一边跑一边叫，从那以后它们就再不敢来偷吃了。这里以前有很多动物，猴子、老虎都很常见。

南岭妇女：以前很艰苦的，没有开公路的时候，都是在山里走

巴黎—卢森堡之行

La route Paris–Luxembourg

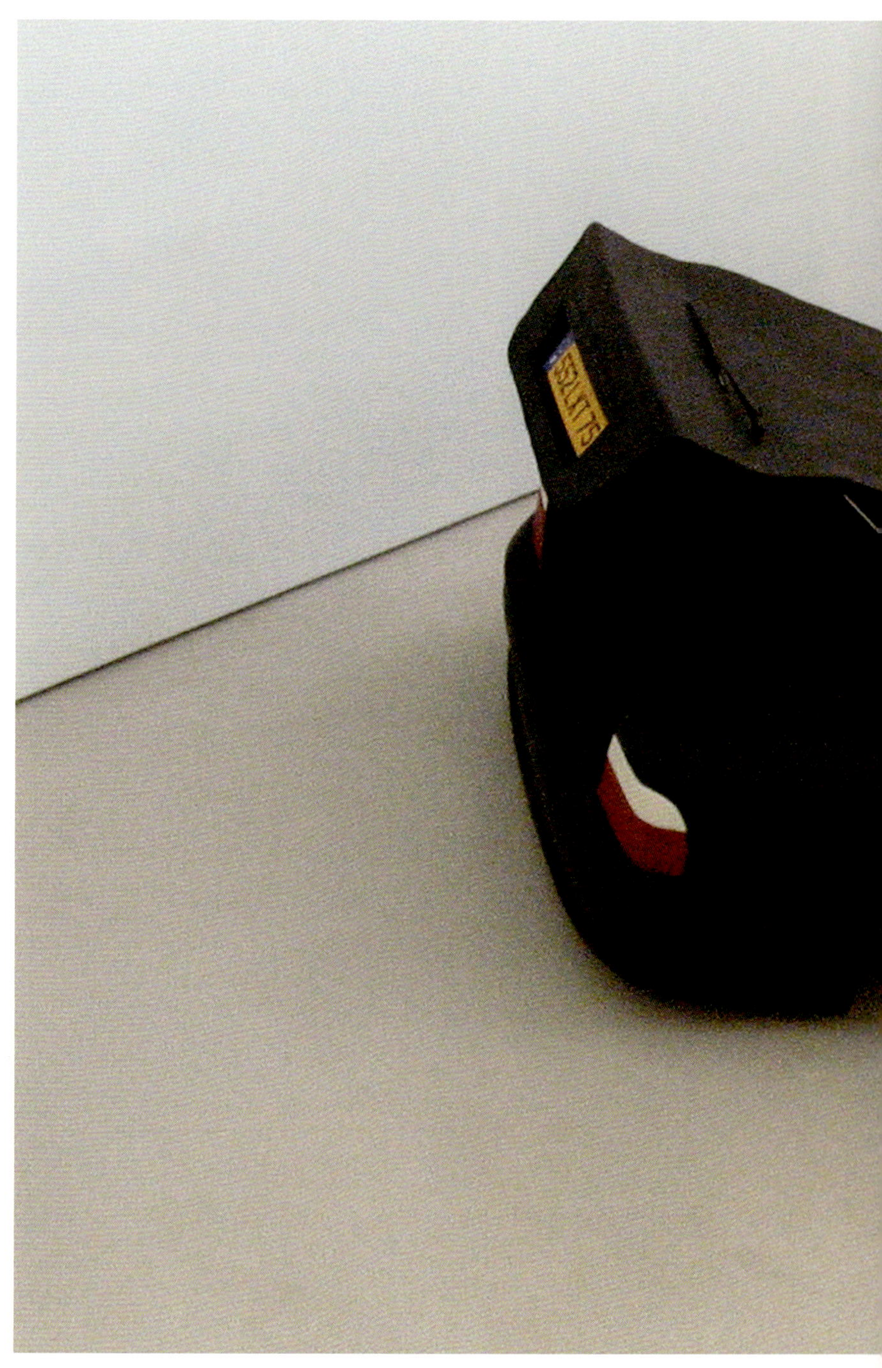

2005年
装置
300×500×150厘米

2005
Installation
300×500×150 cm

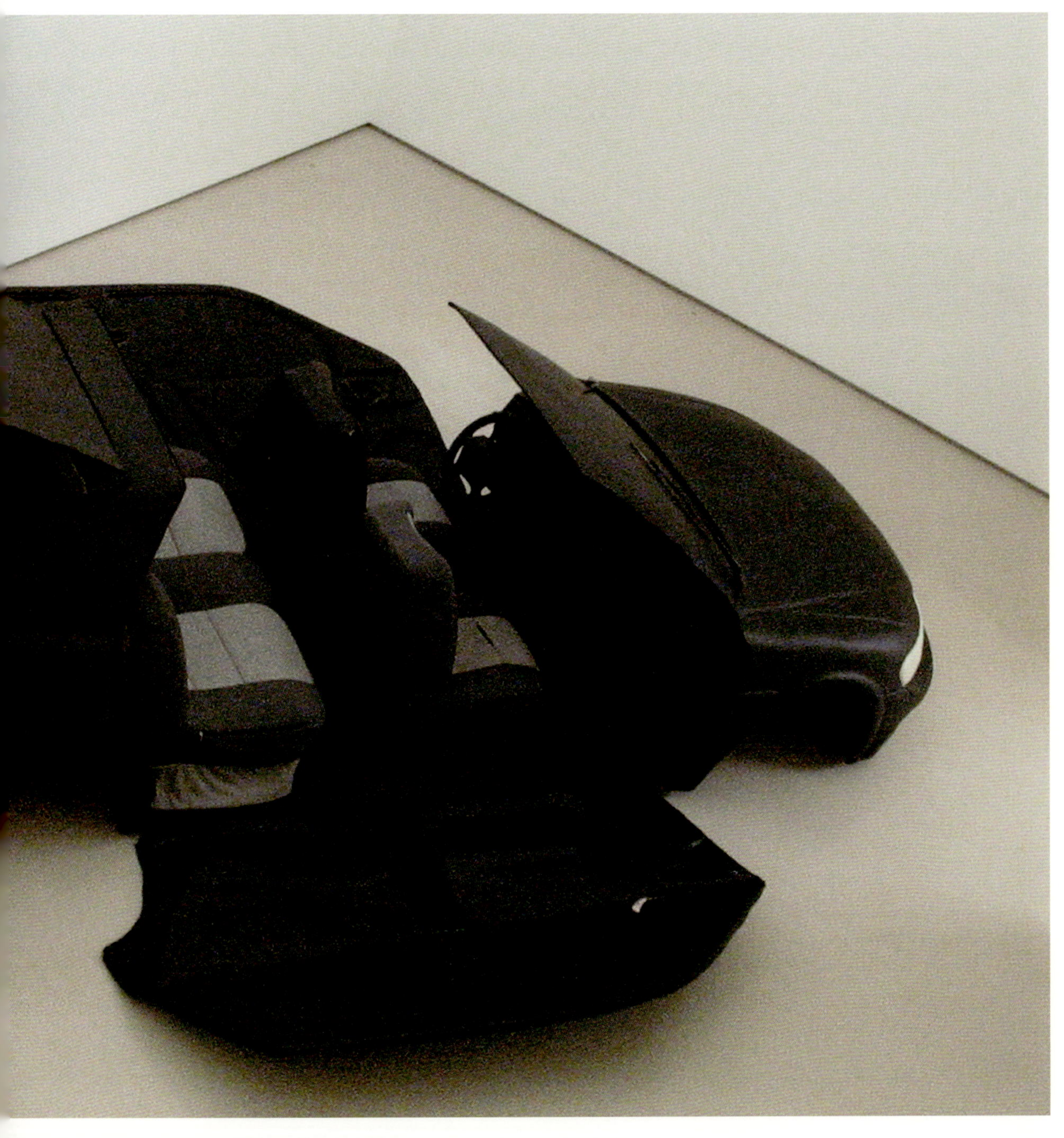

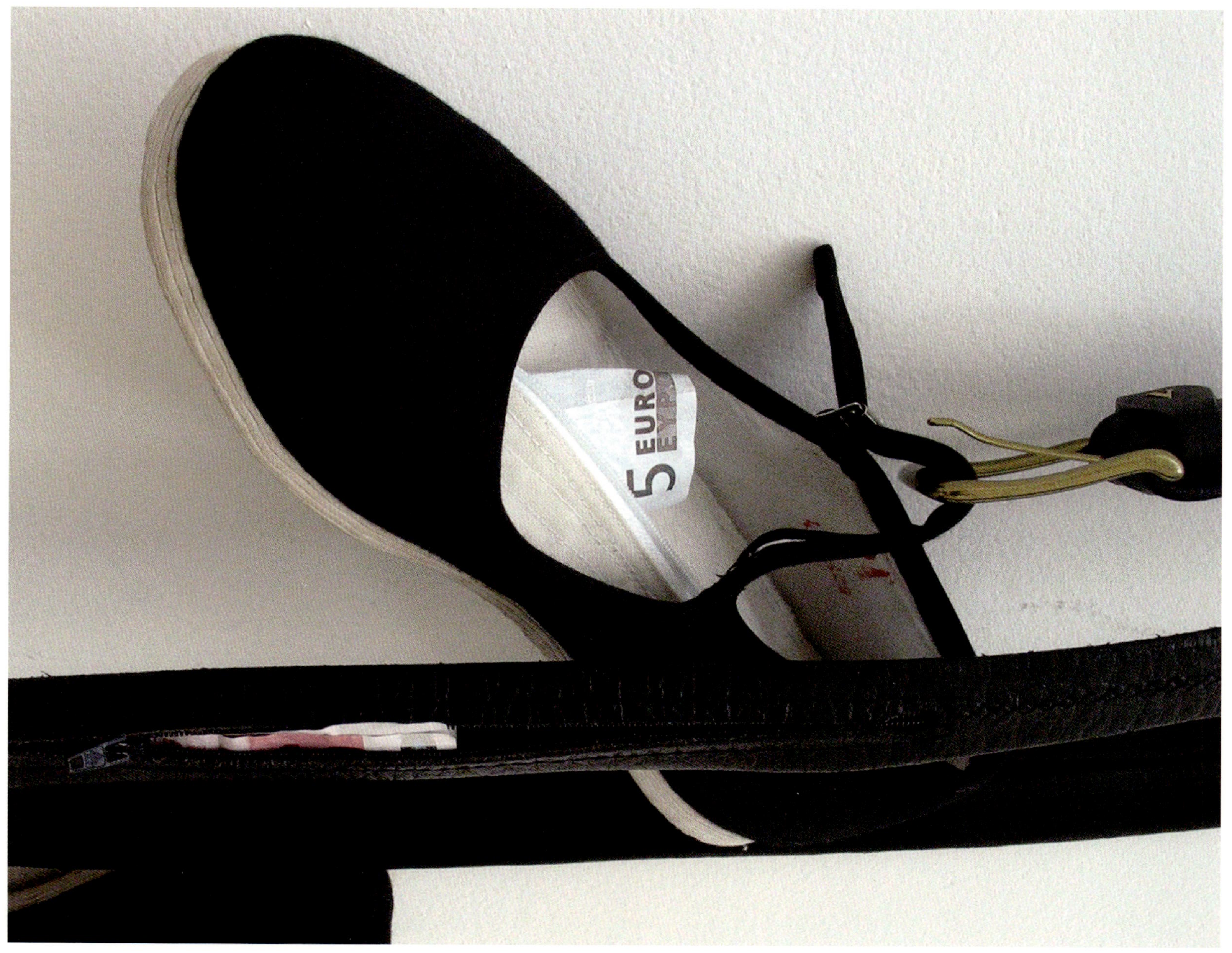
5 EURO
EYPΩ

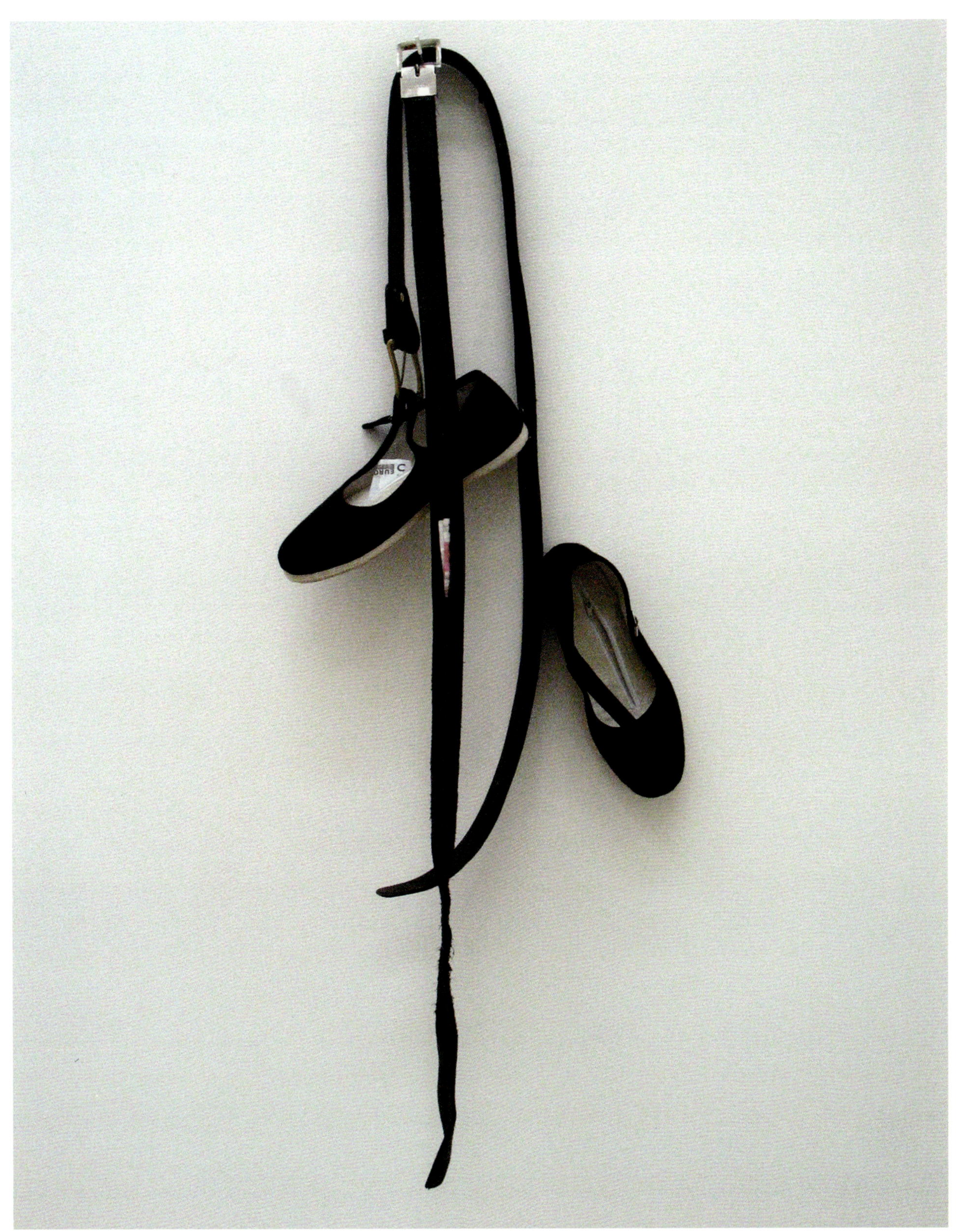

南国长城
The Great Wall in Southern China

2005年
装置
800×700×150厘米

2005
Installation
800×700×150 cm

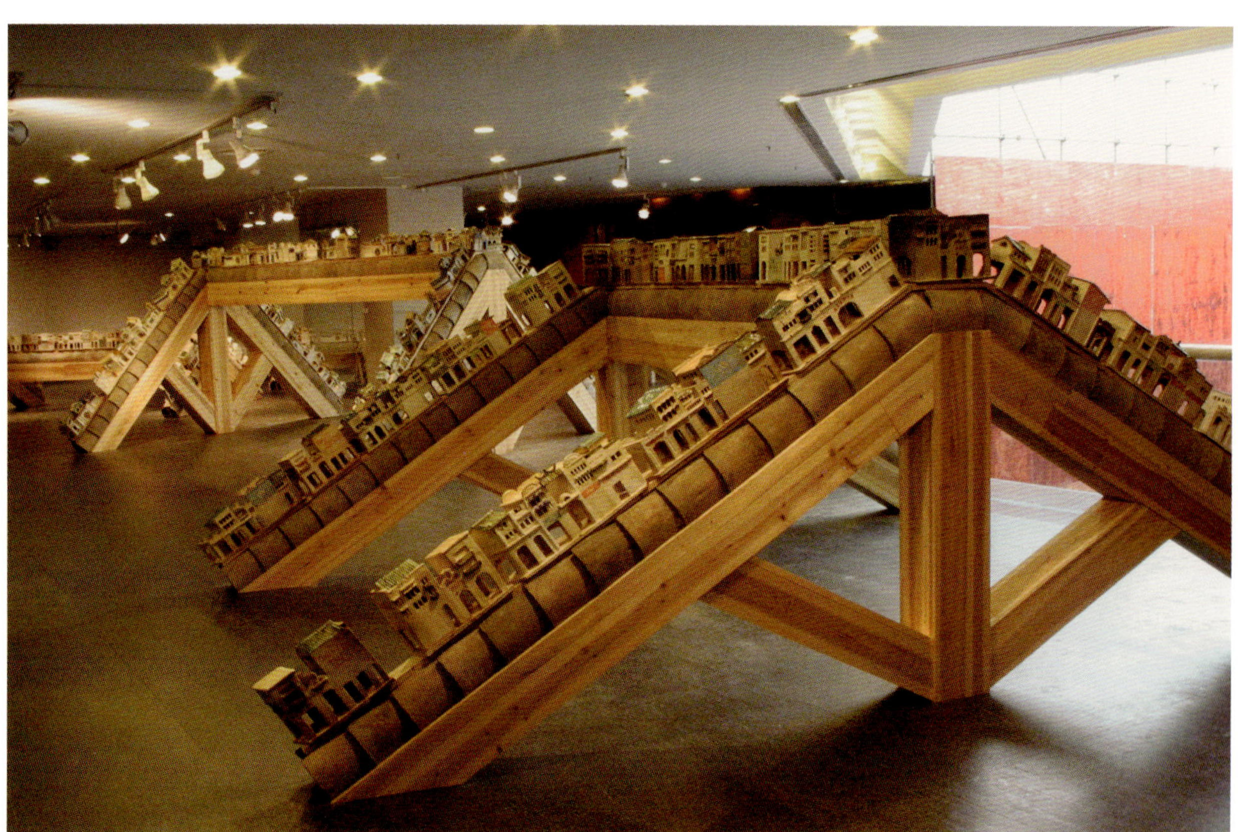

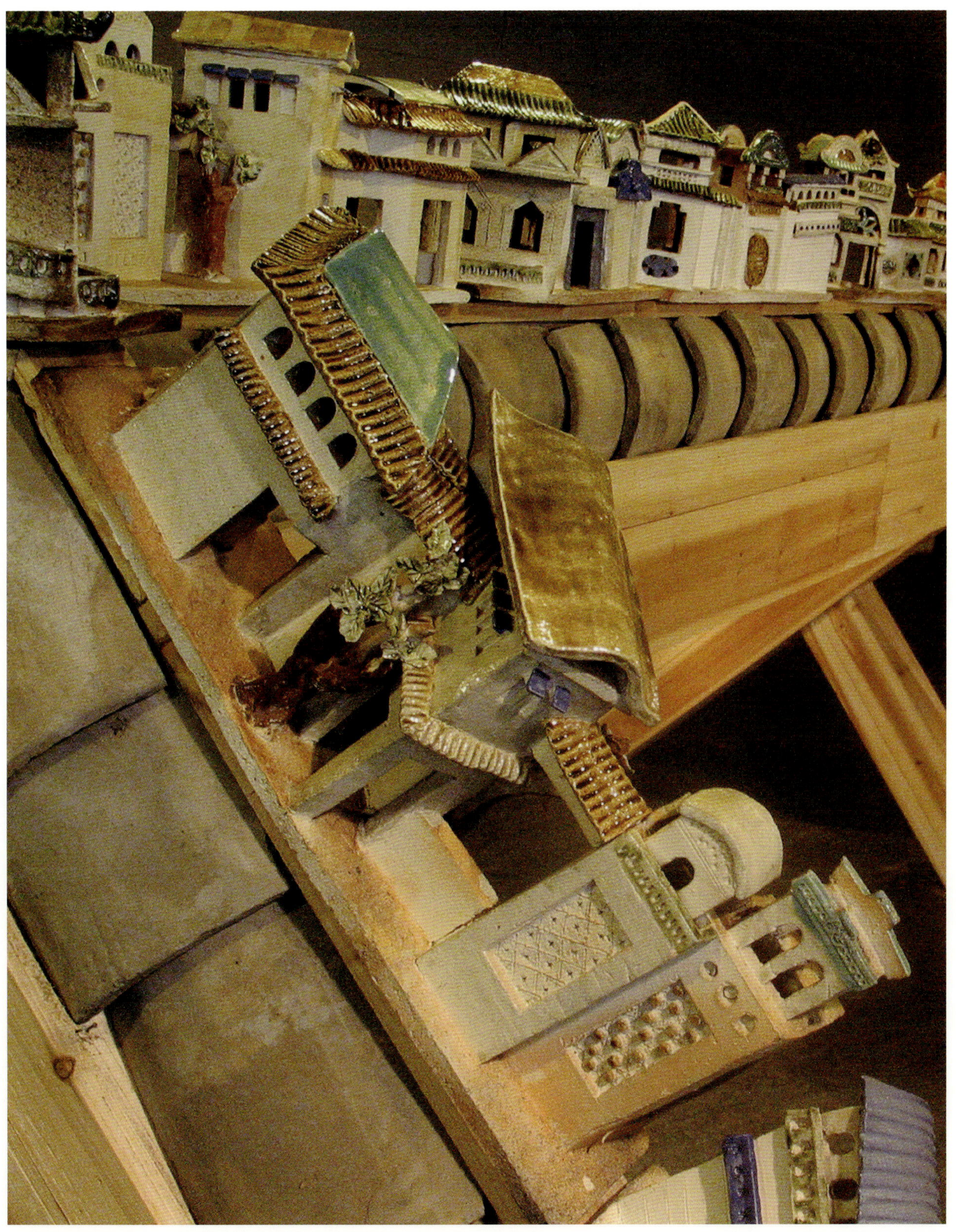

桥
Bridge

2004年
装置
1000×100×300厘米

2004
Installation
1000×100×300 cm

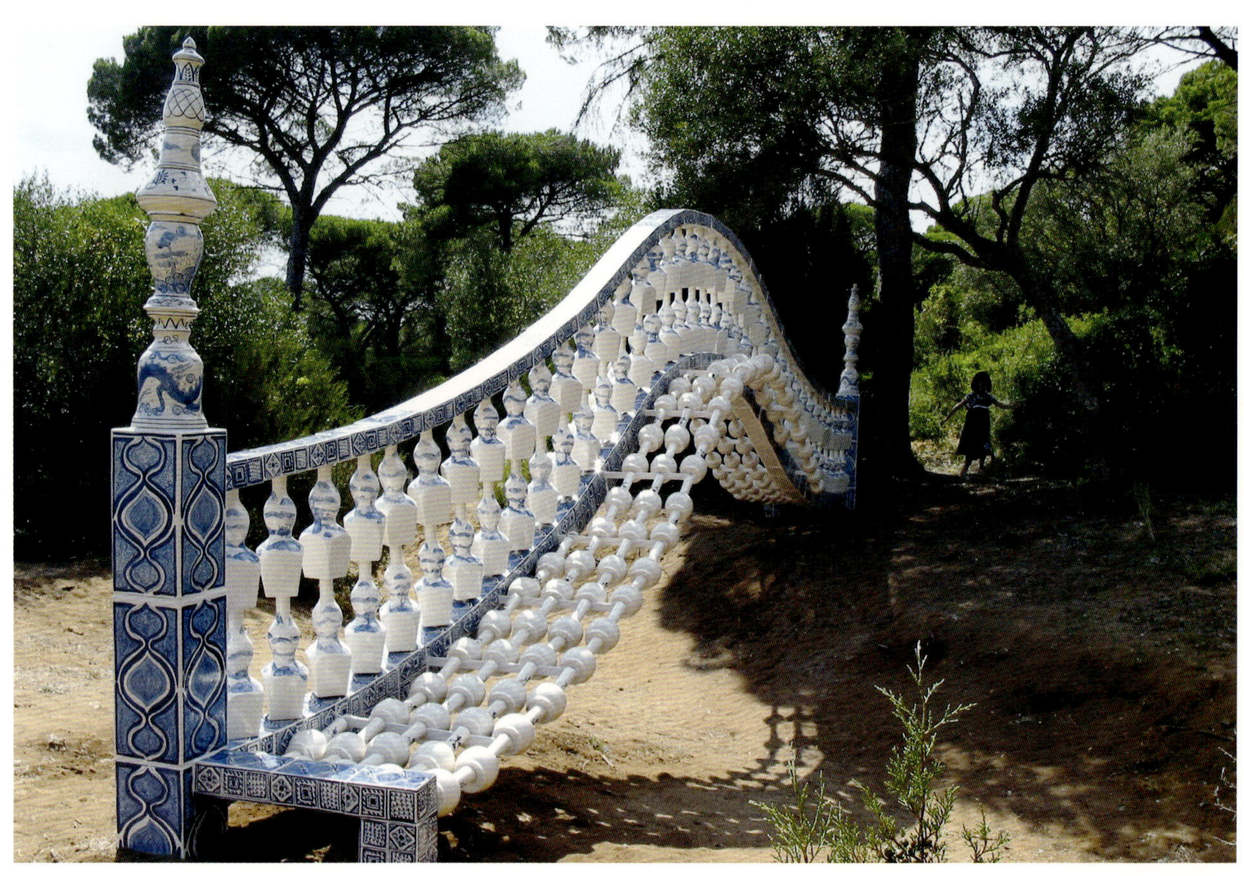

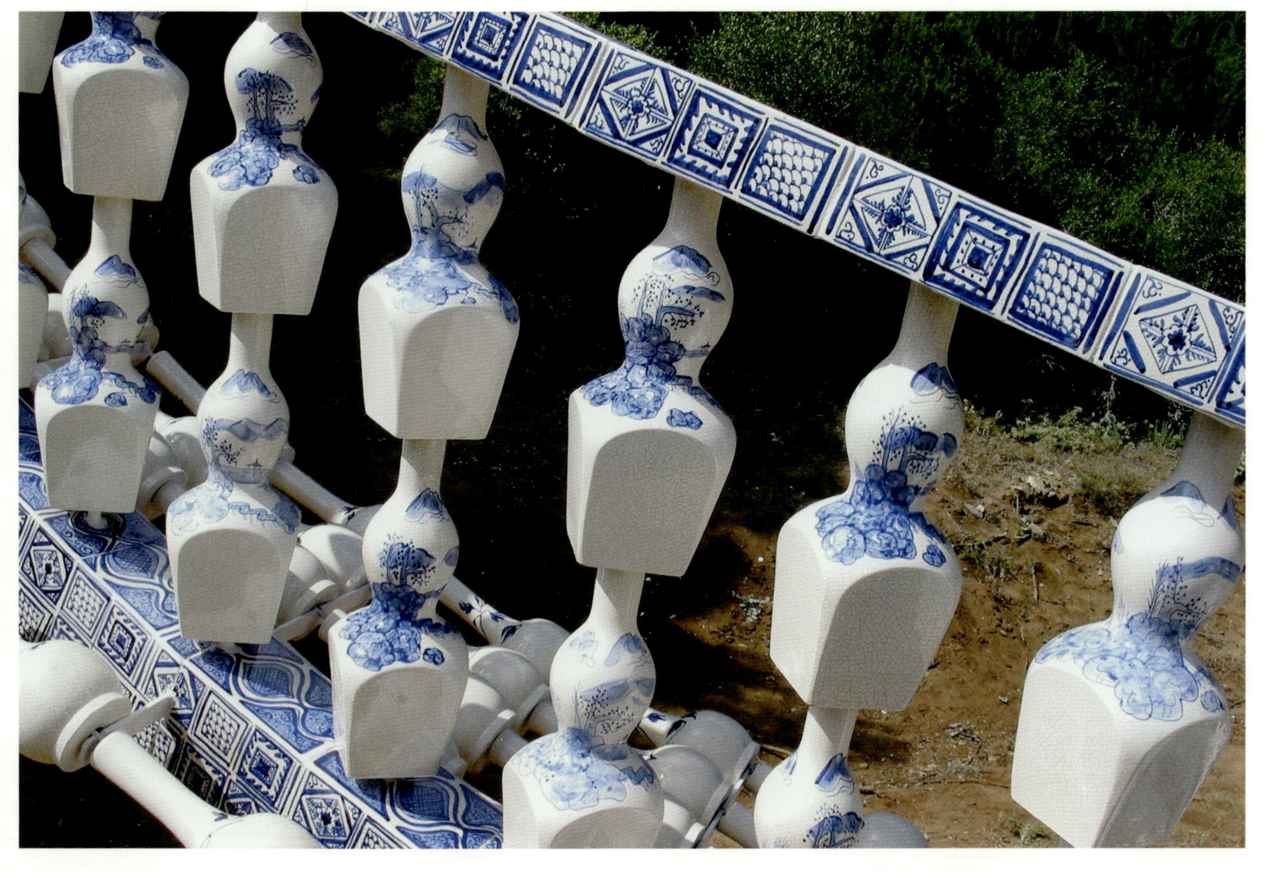

蓝色公路
Blue Freeway

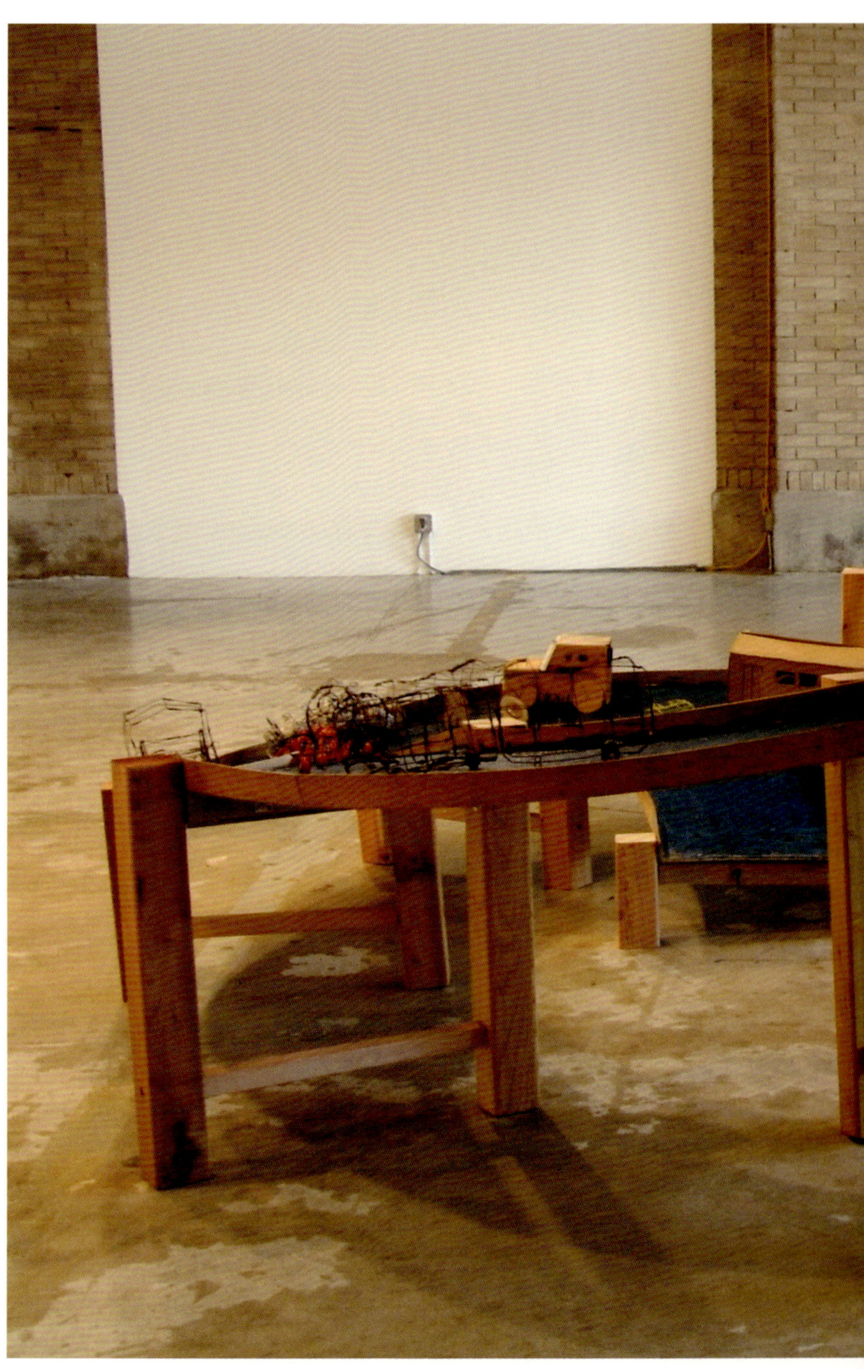

2004年
装置
1000×100×300厘米

2004
Installation
1000×100×300 cm

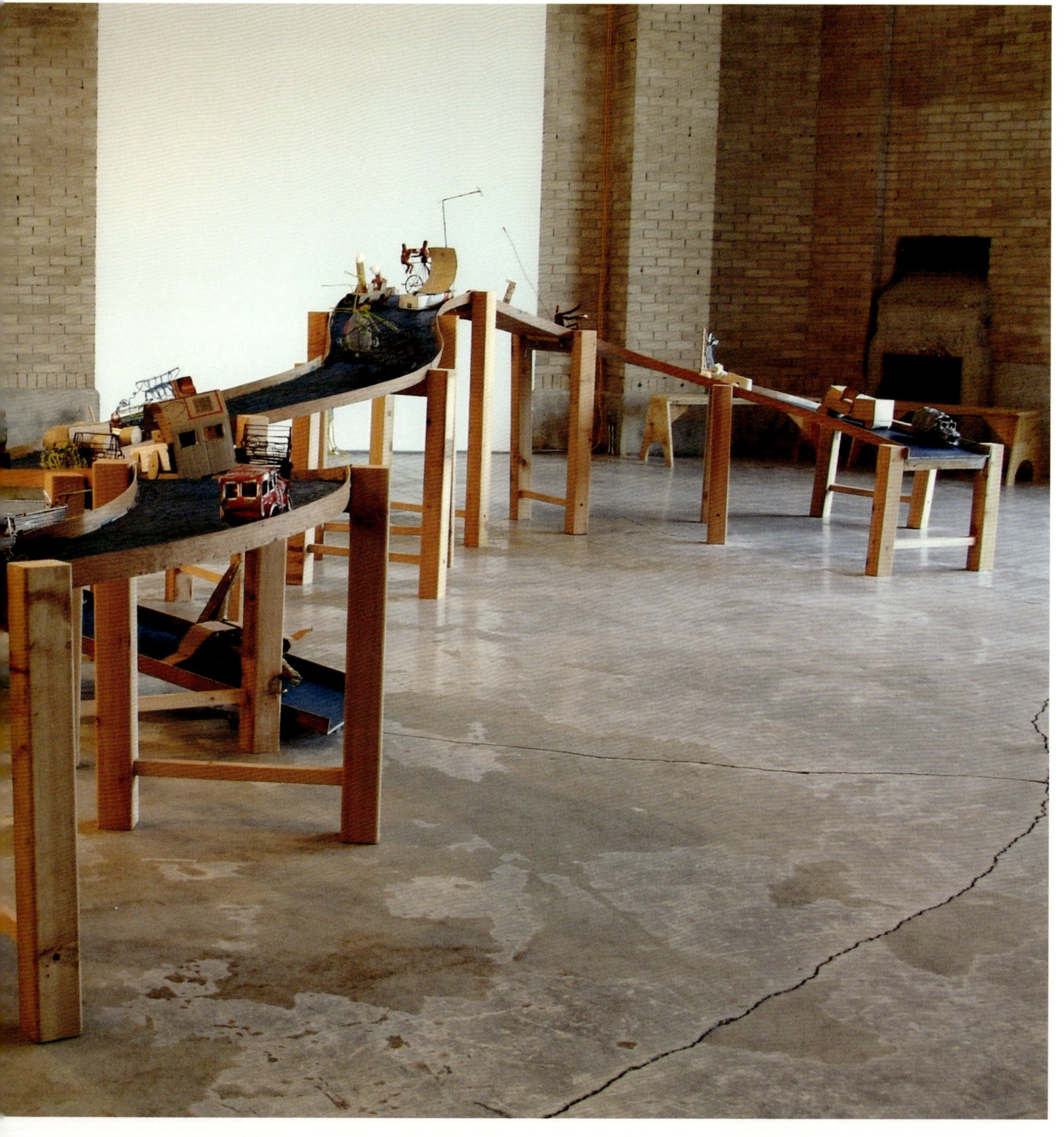

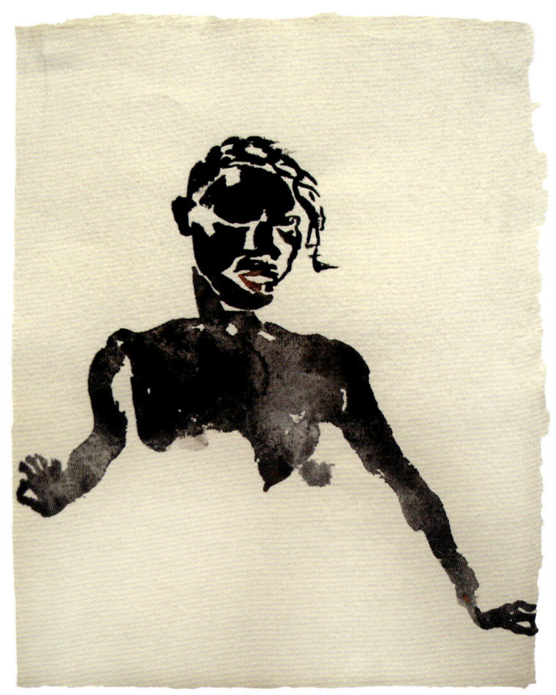
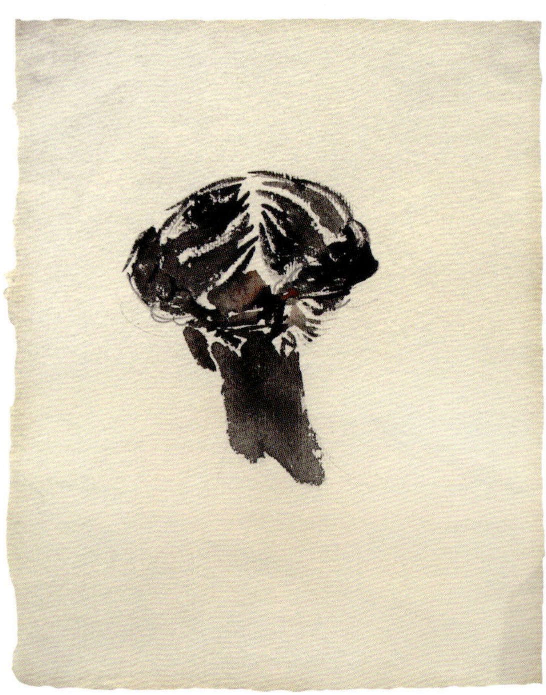
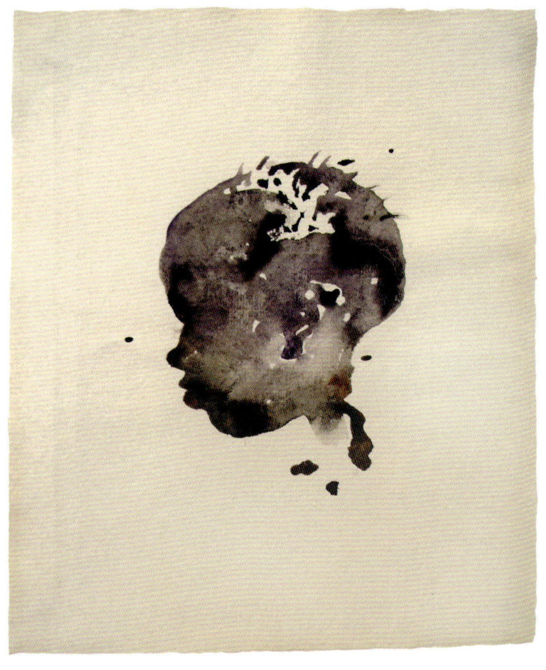
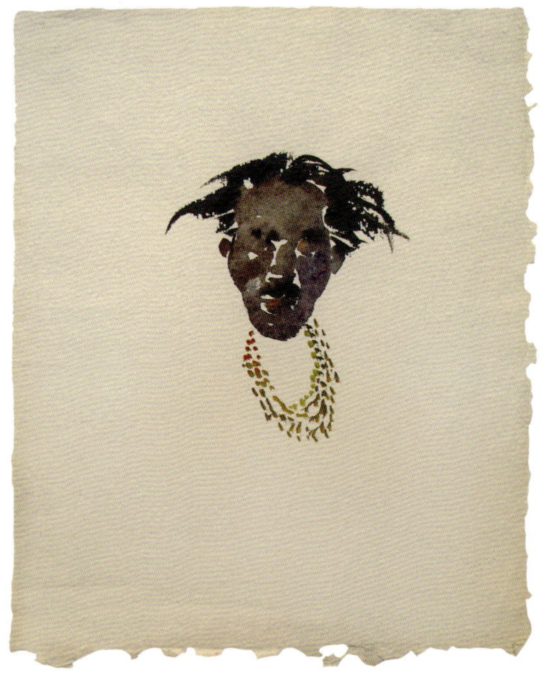

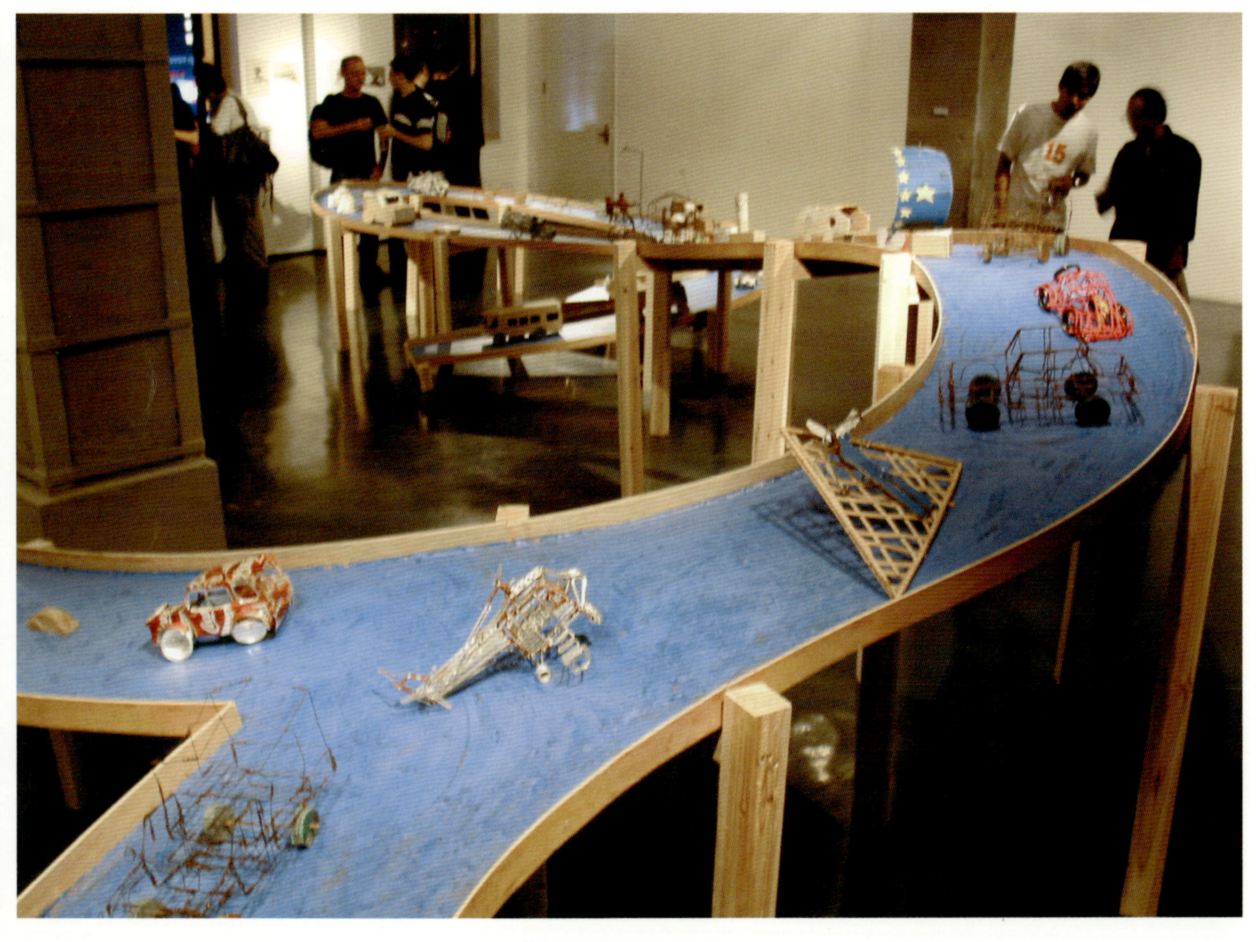

飞碗

Flying Bowl

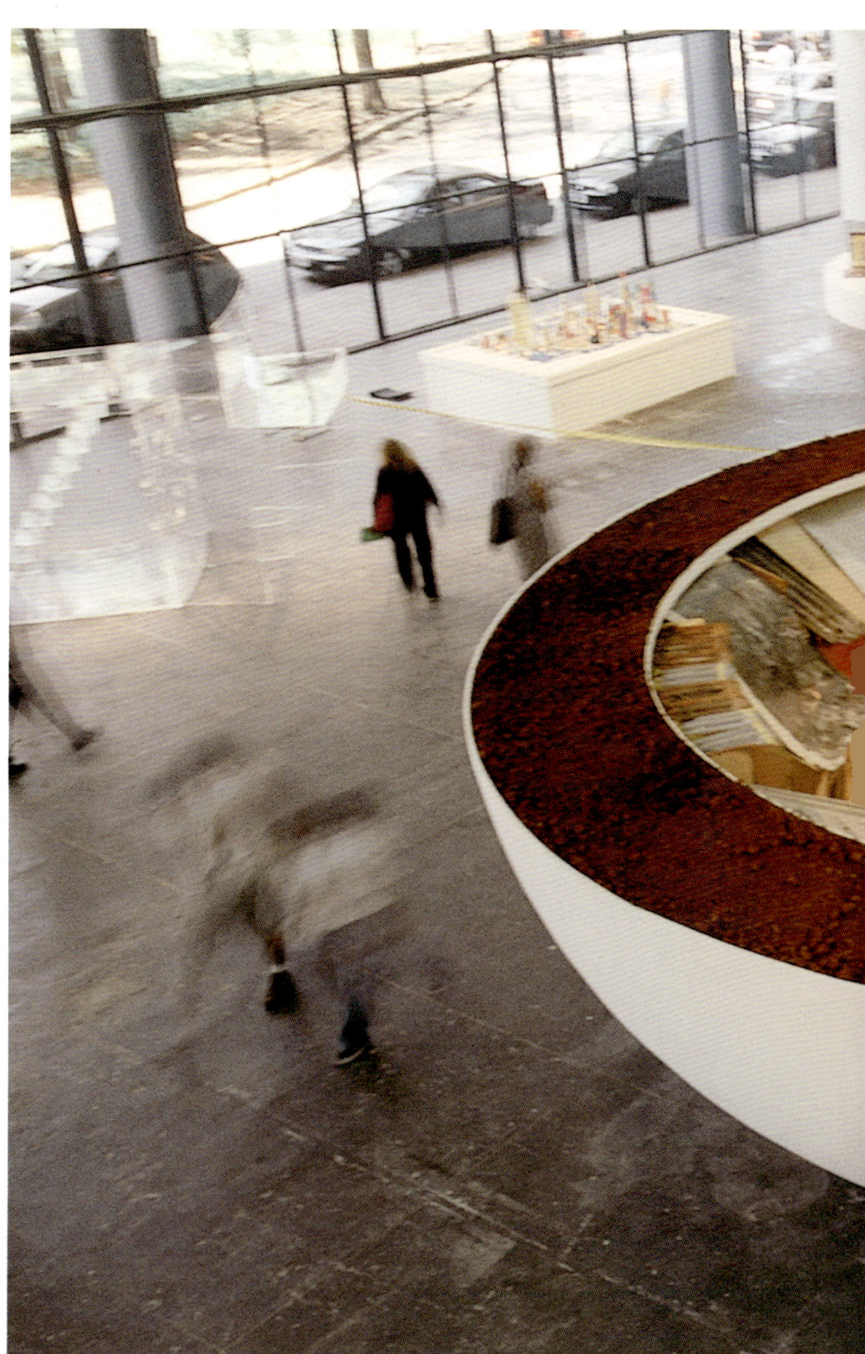

2002年
装置
800×800×270厘米

2002
Installation
800×800×270 cm

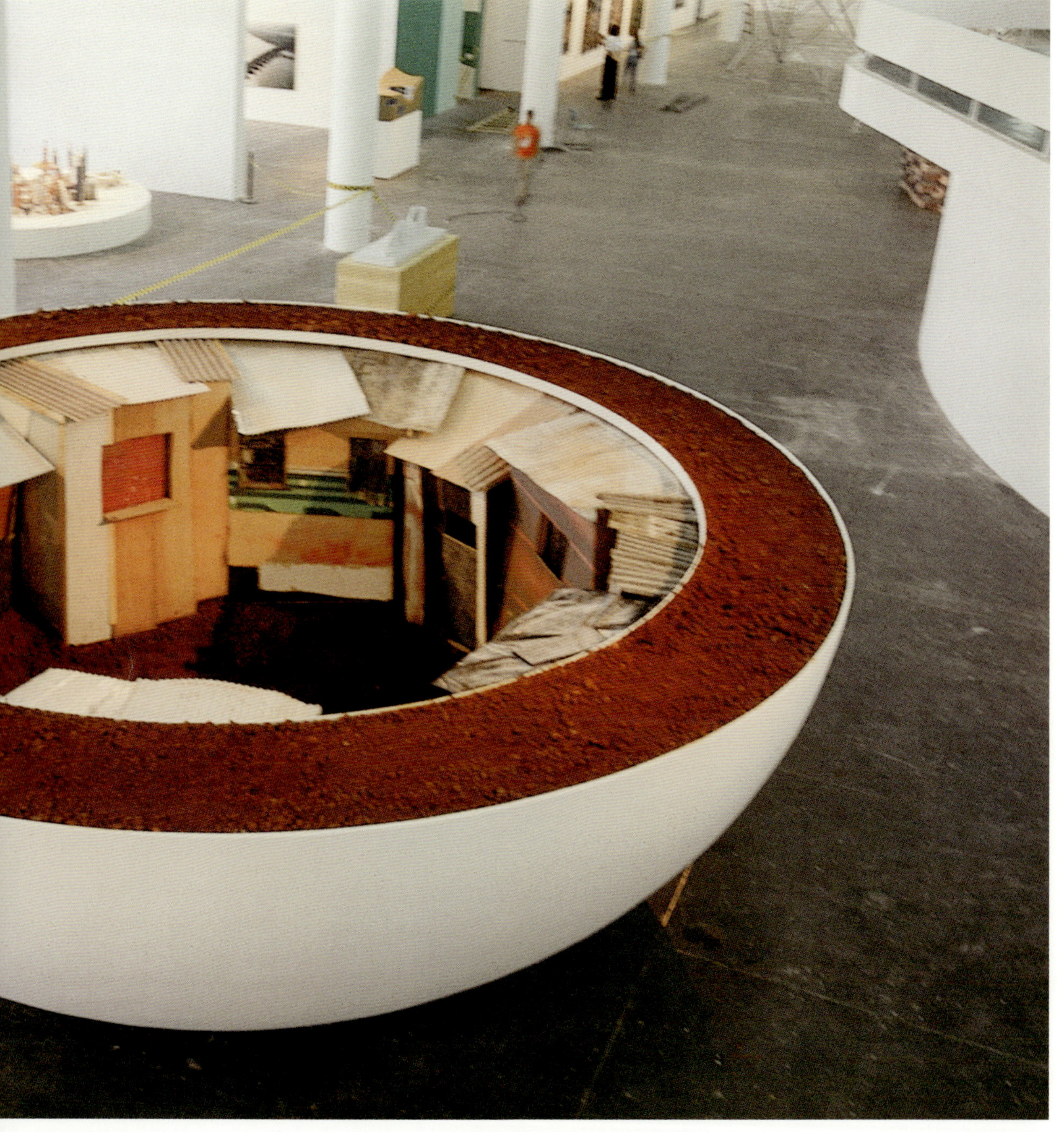

白费口舌

Perdre sa salive

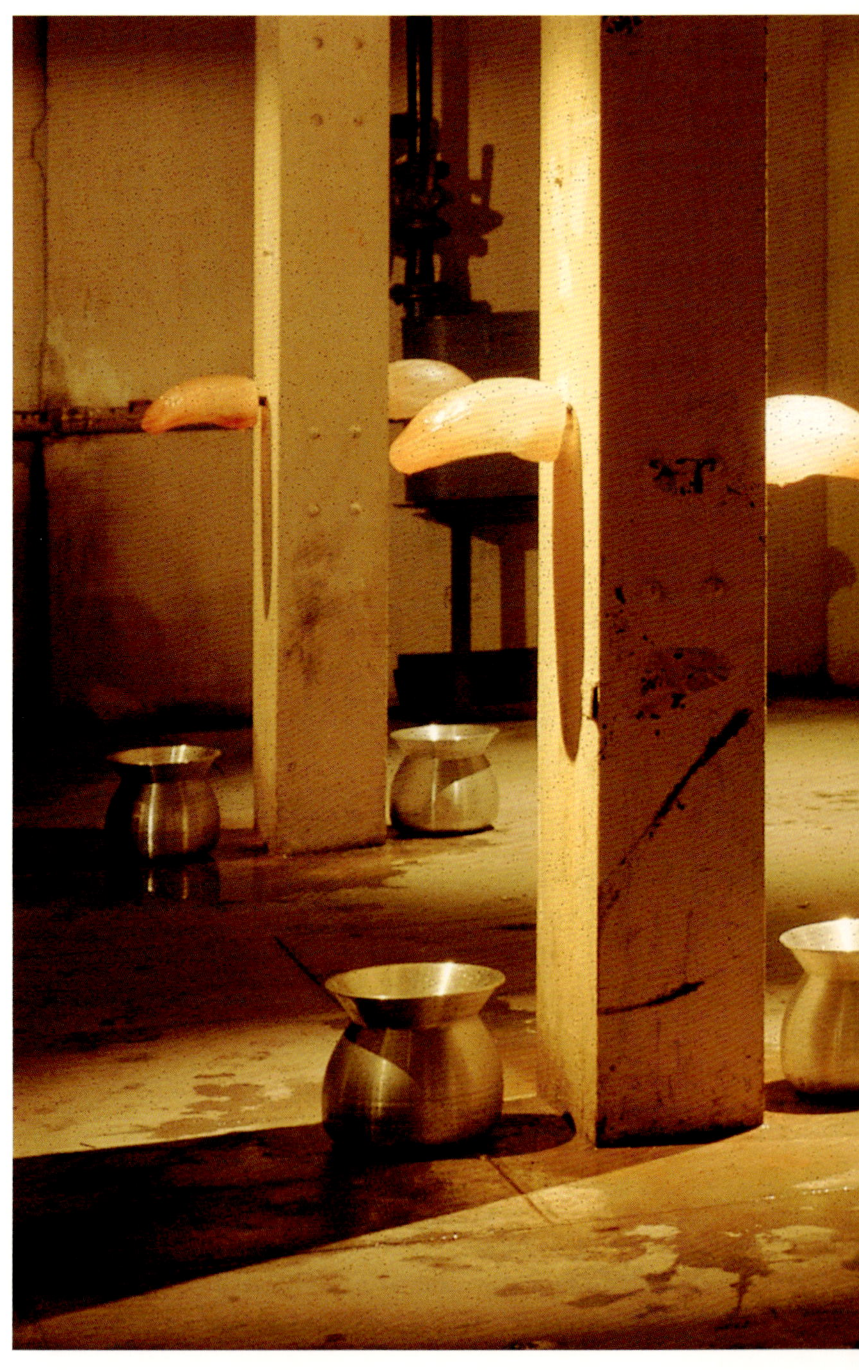

1994年
装置
可变尺寸

1994
Installation
Dimensions variable

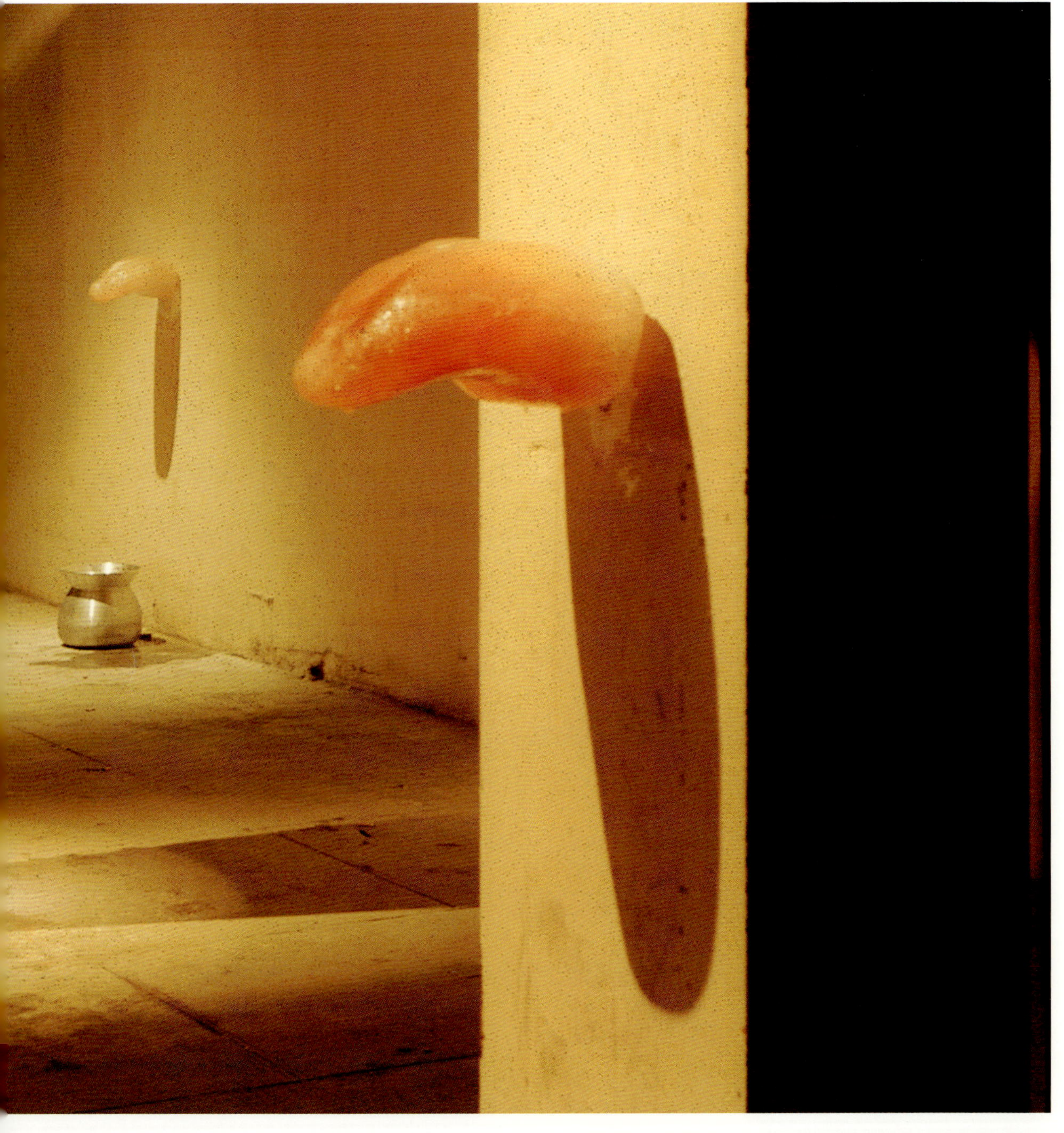

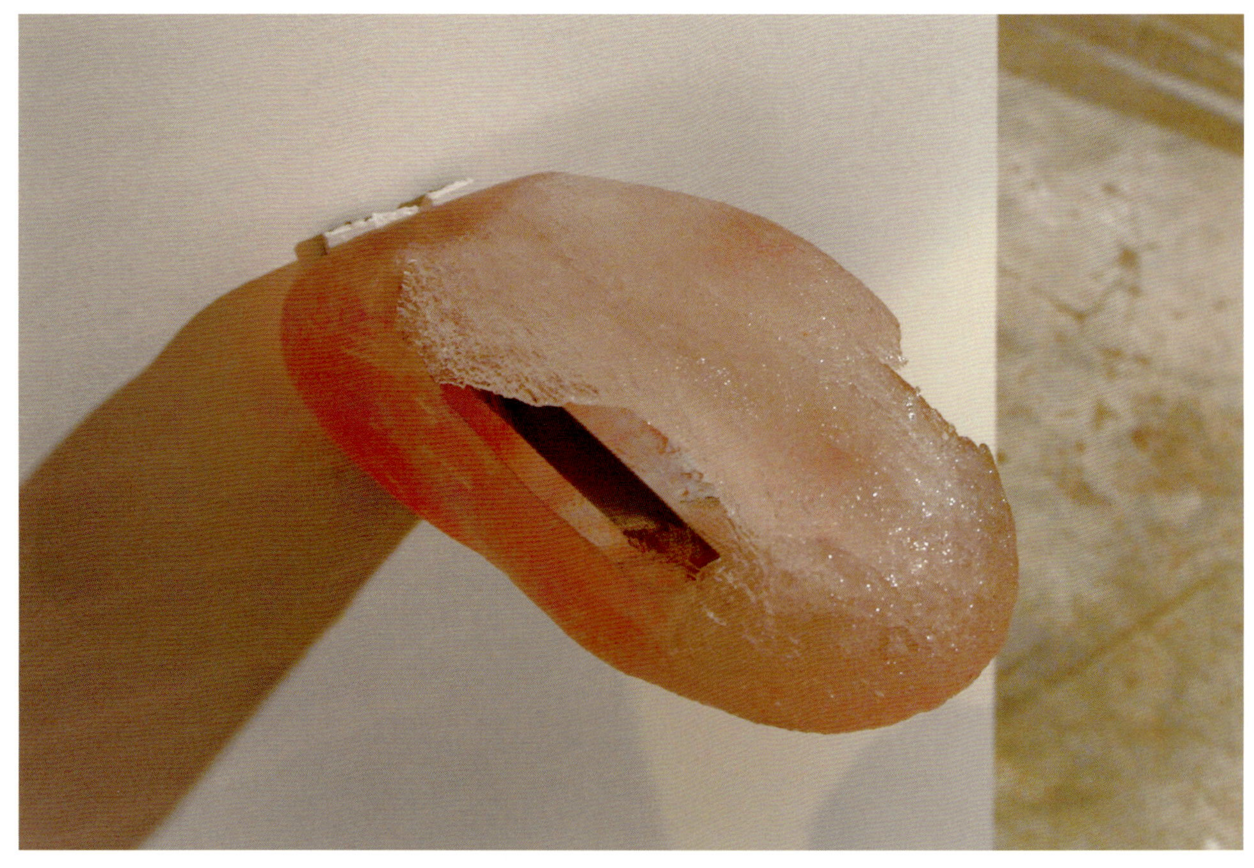

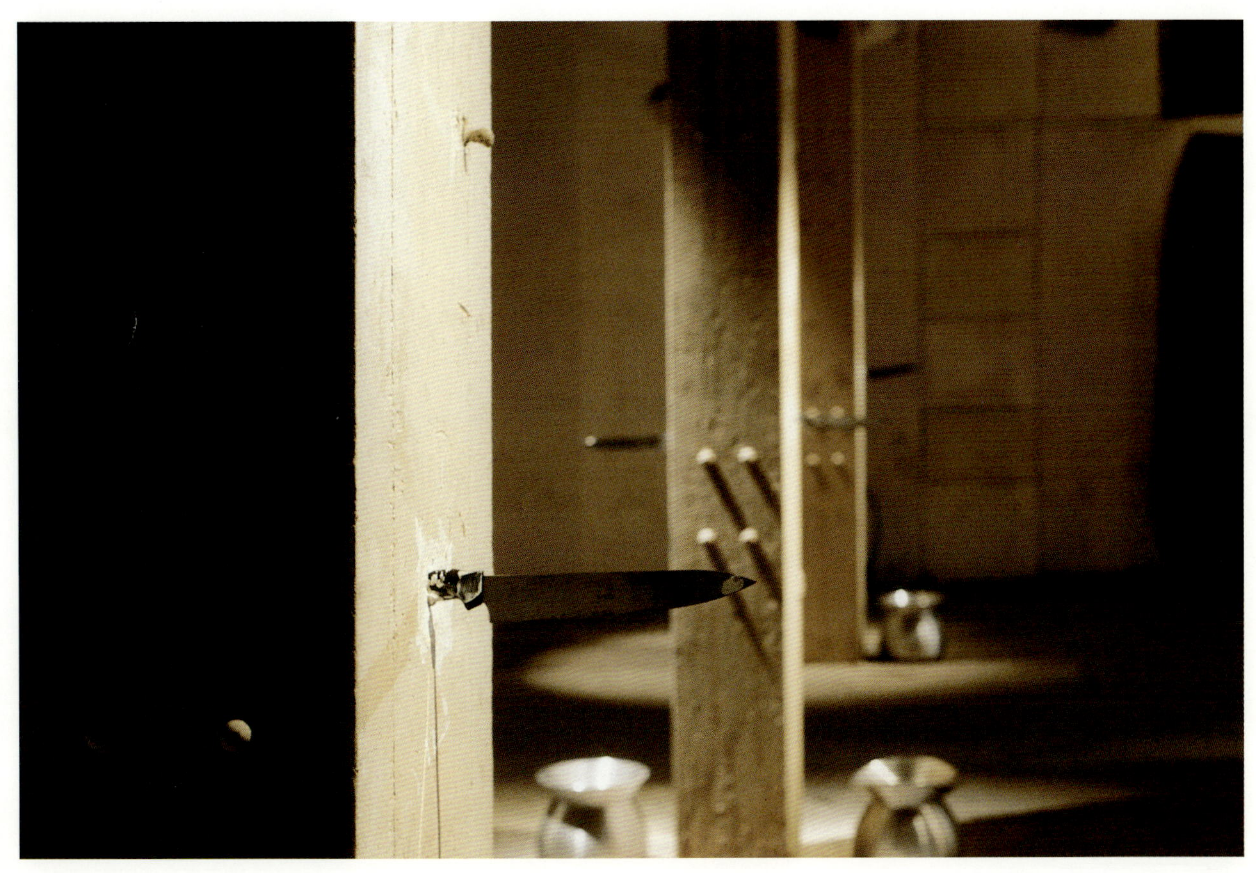

三五成群

In Threes and Fours, or in Knots

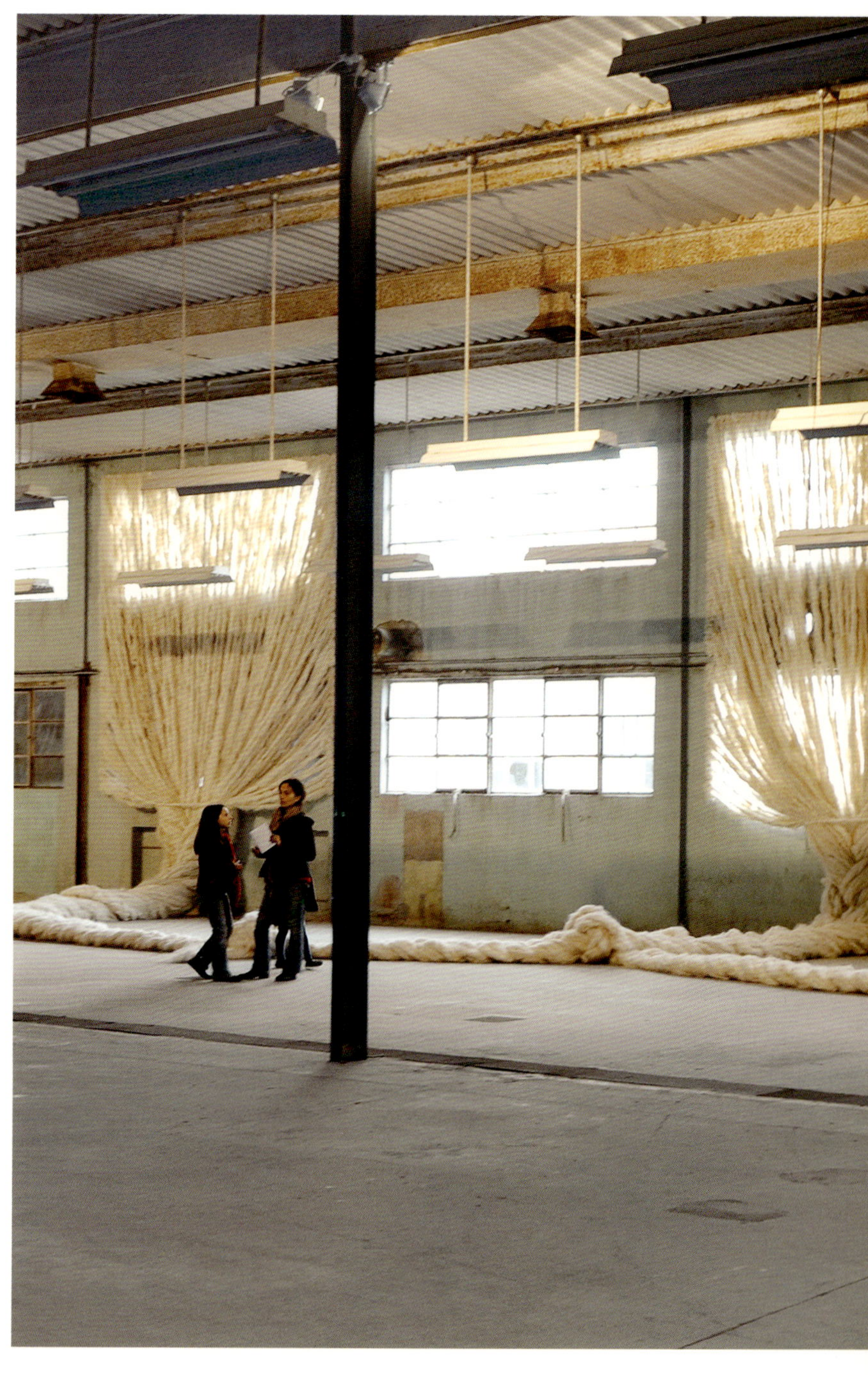

1997—2008年
装置
可变尺寸

1997 – 2008
Installation
Dimensions variable

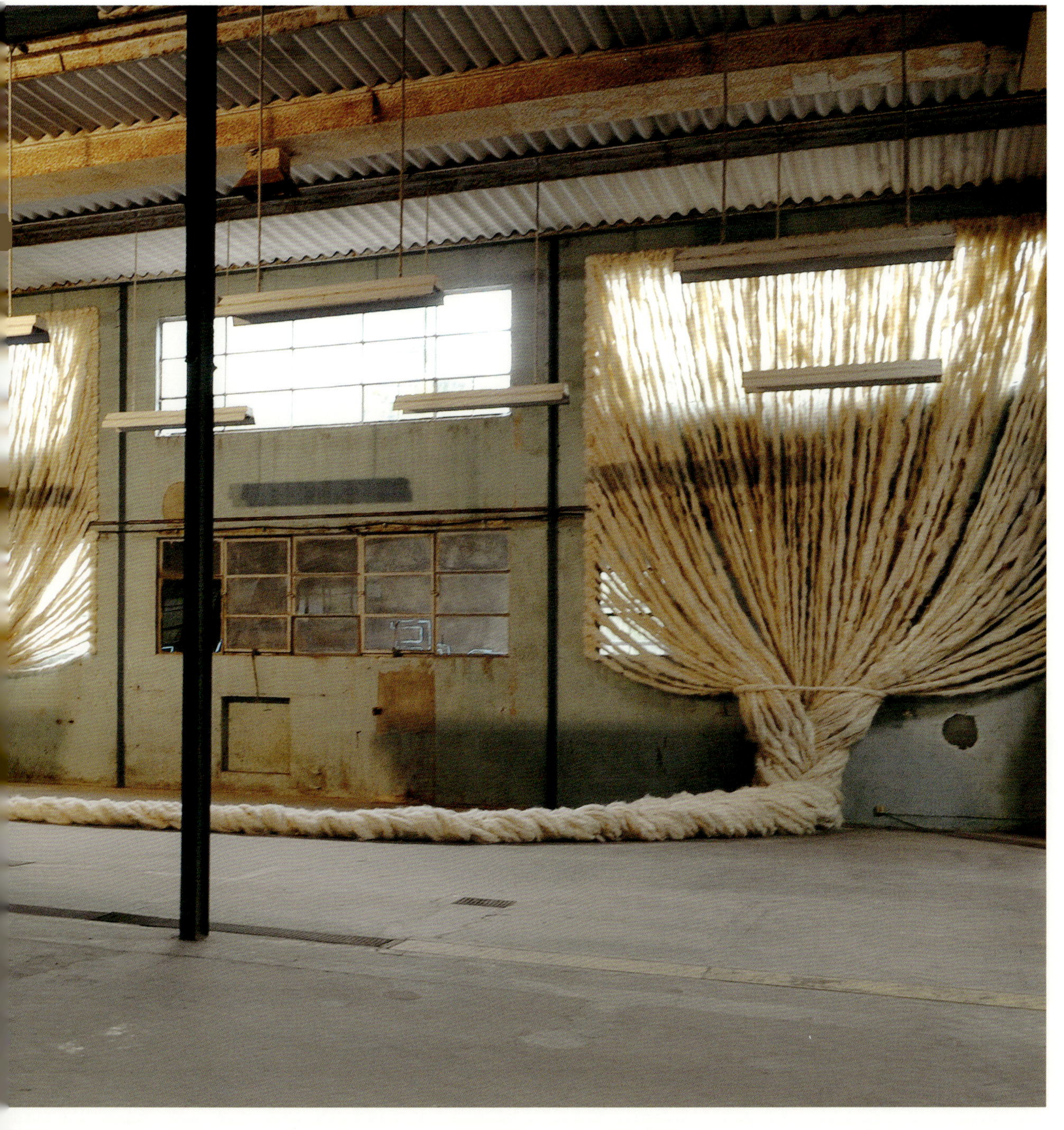

跳床
Trampoline

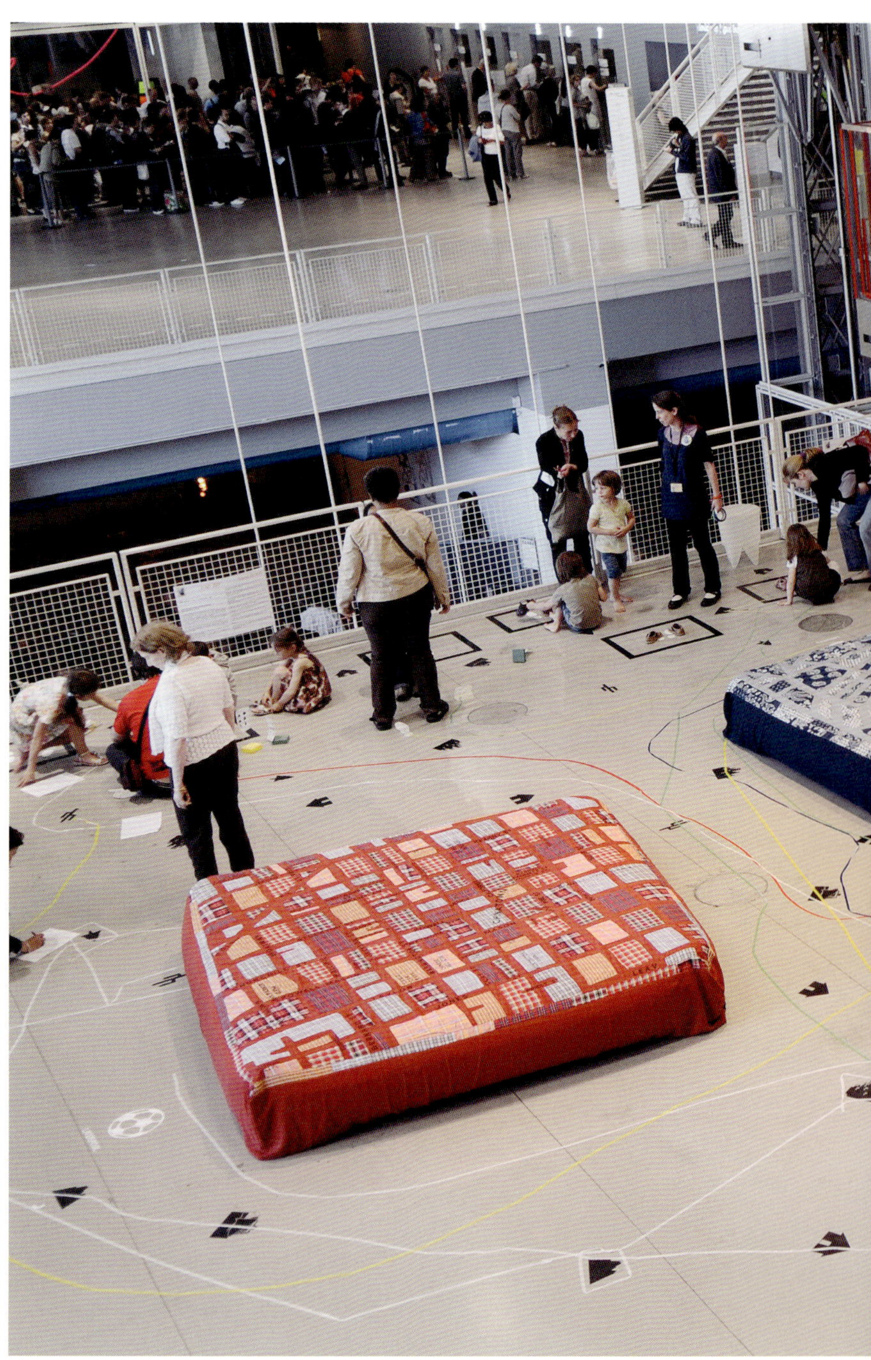

2004—2009年
装置
200×200×40厘米×5

2004 – 2009
Installation
200×200×40 cm×5

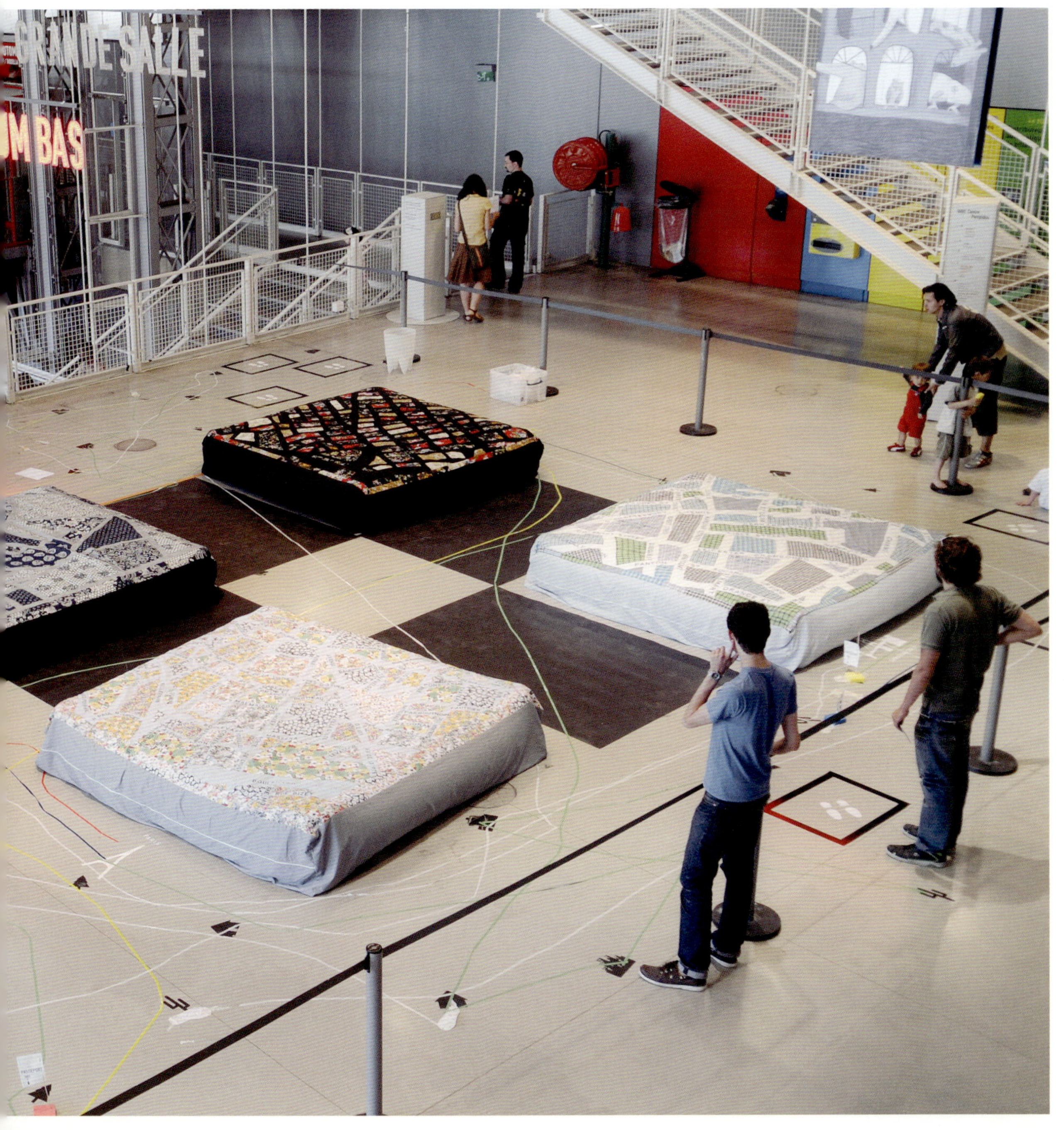

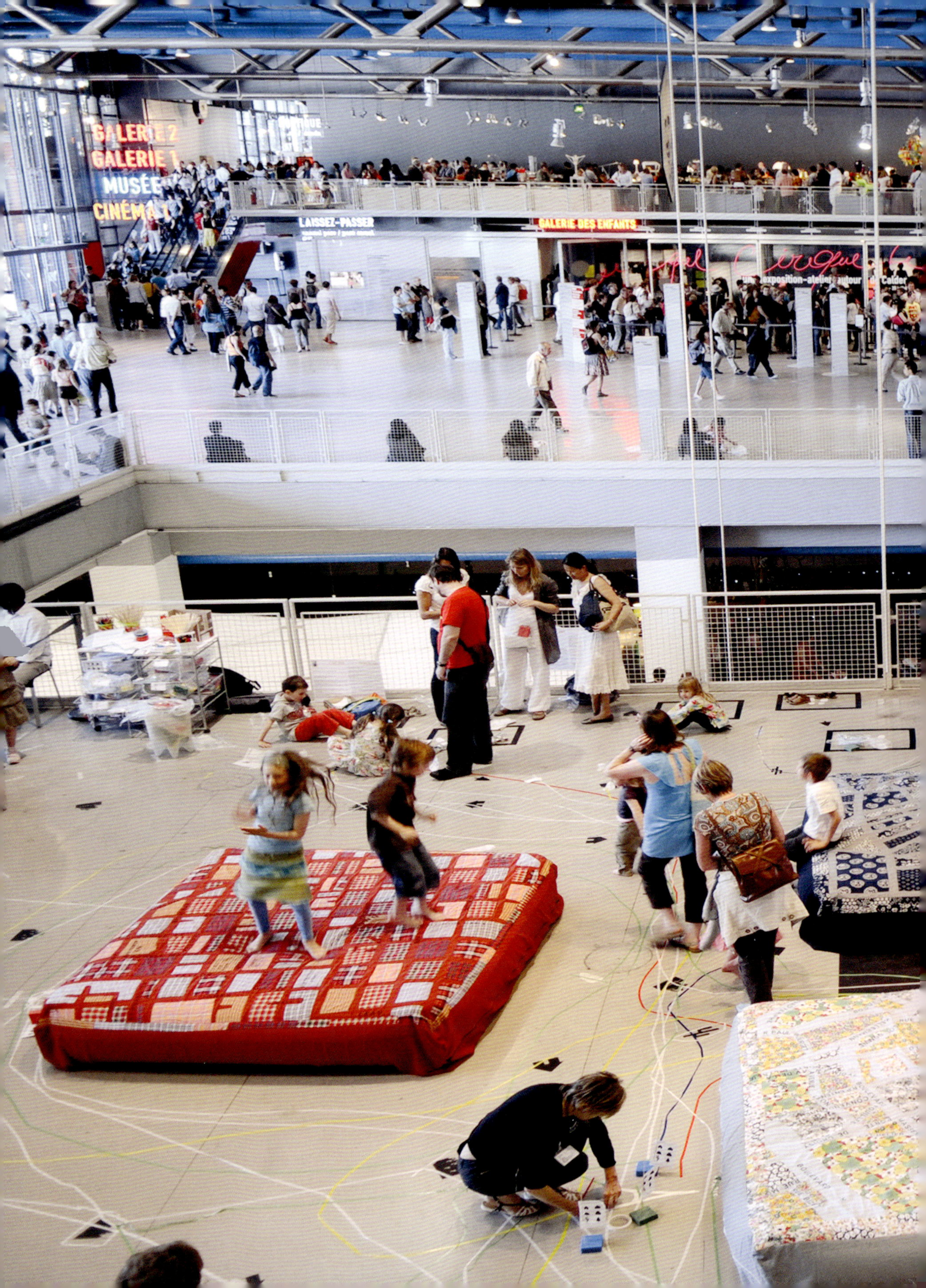

GALERIE 2
GALERIE 1
MUSÉE
CINÉMA 1
LAISSEZ-PASSER
GALERIE DES ENFANTS

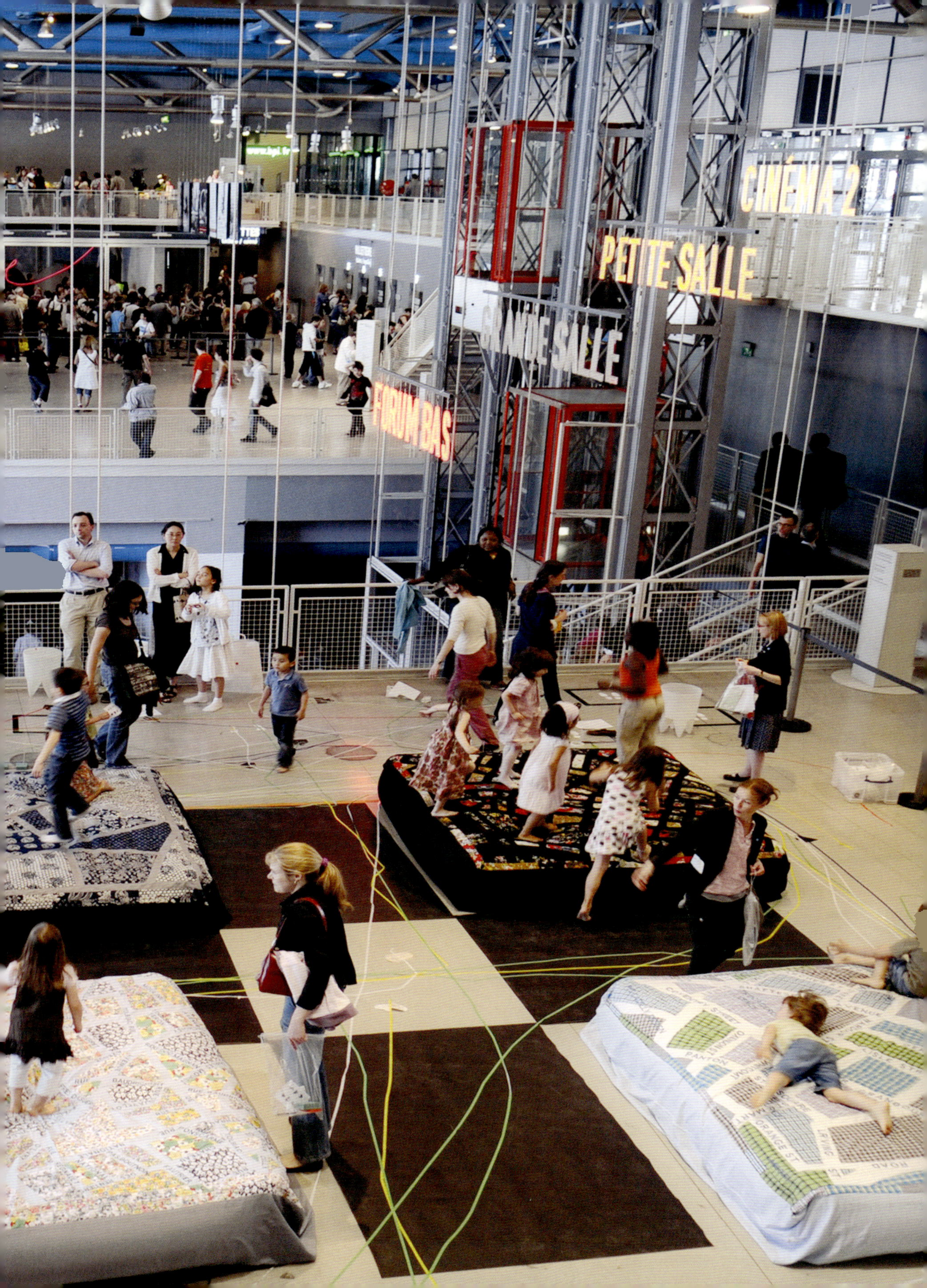

CINÉMA 2
PETITE SALLE
GRANDE SALLE
FORUM BAS

水床 1
Eau-lit-1

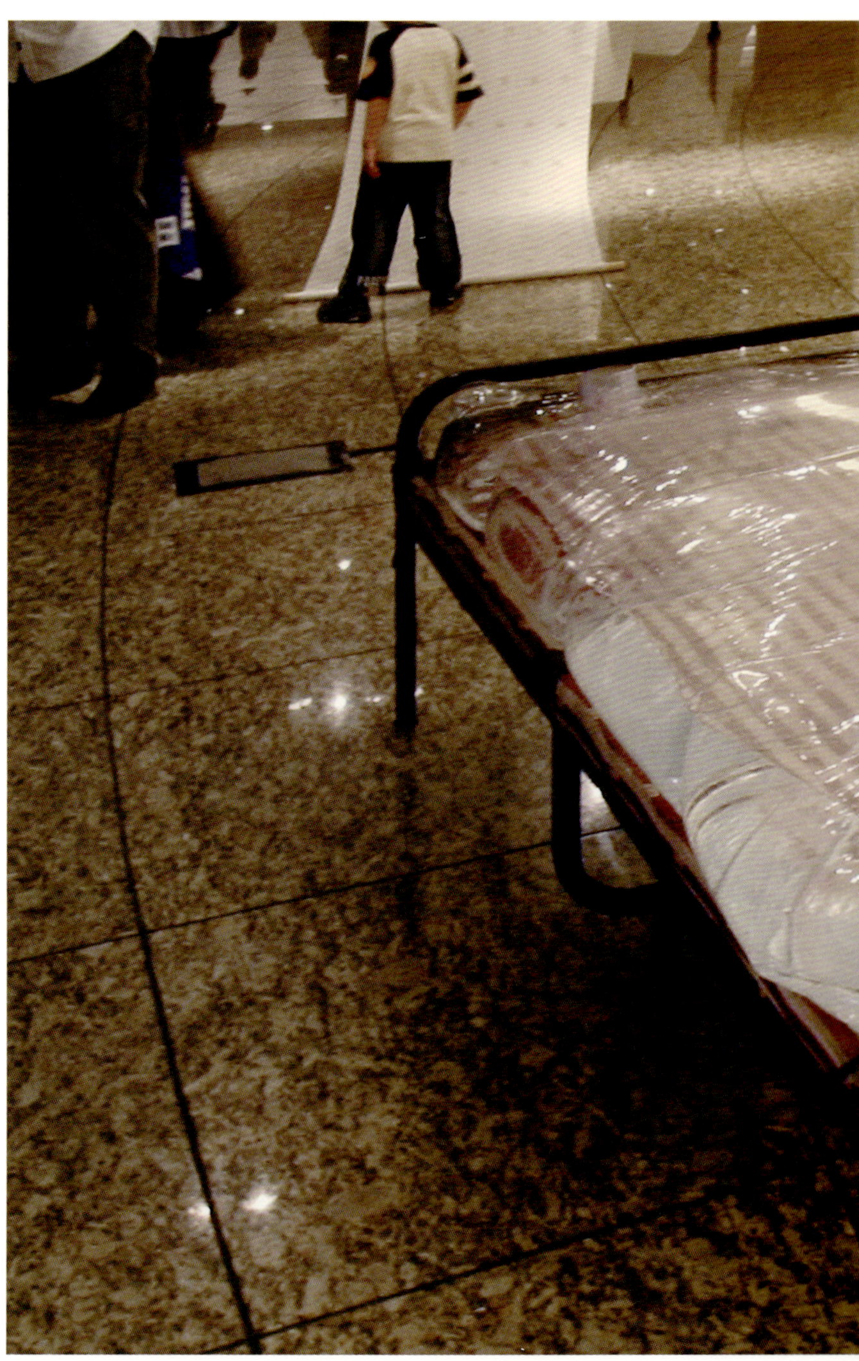

1989—2005年
装置
200×250×300厘米

1989 – 2005
Installation
200×250×300 cm

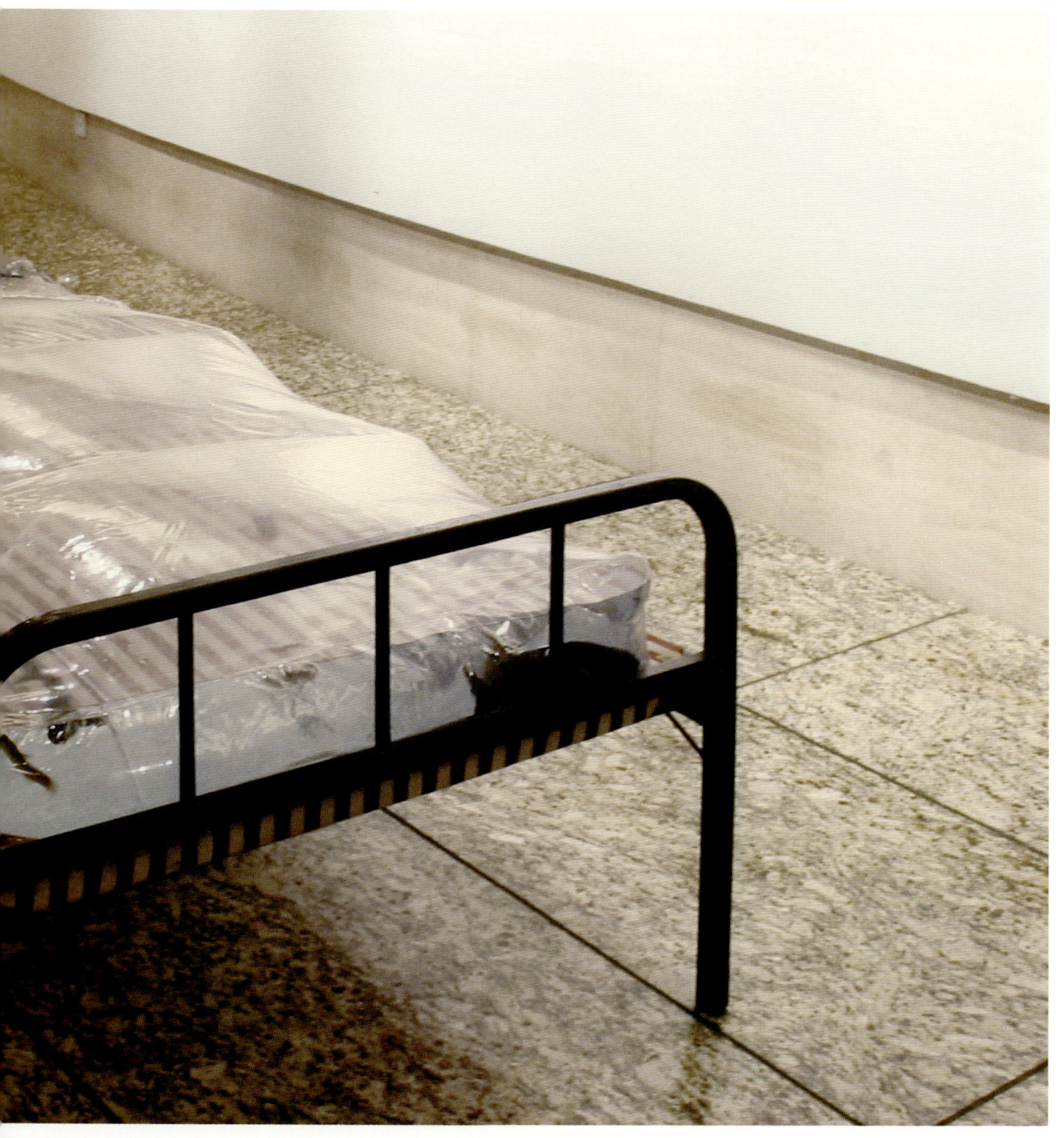

水床 2
Eau-lit-2

2007年
装置
200×250×300厘米

2007
Installation
200×250×300 cm

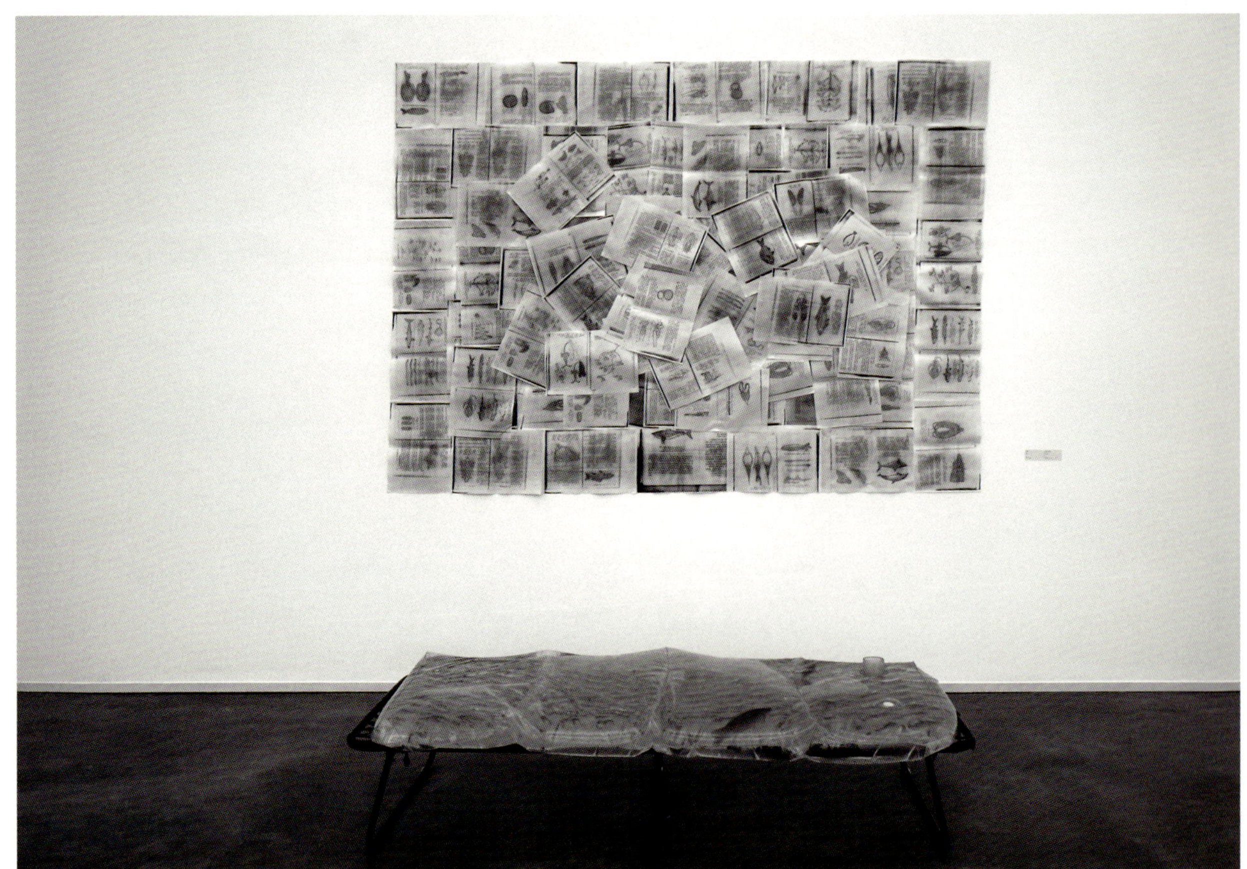

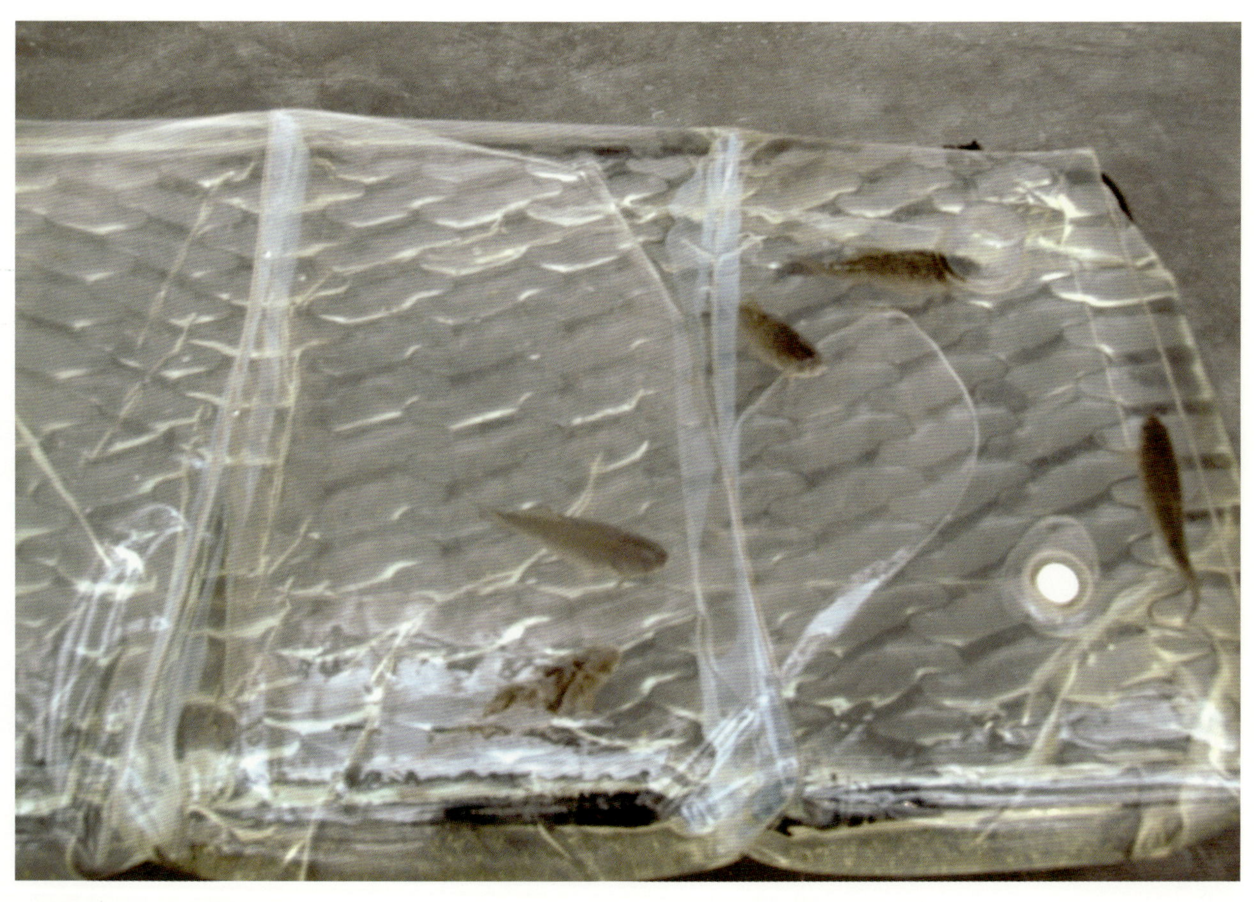

迁徙的身份：对沈远的访谈

The Migrating Identity:
In Conversation with Shen Yuan

杰罗姆·桑斯
尤伦斯当代艺术中心馆长

JÉRÔME SANS
Director,
Ullens Center for Contemporary Art

Jérôme Sans: What did the Xiamen Dada movement of the 1980s mean for you?

Shen Yuan: I was only an observer, I did not actually participate. I have always had my own work; Yong Ping and I try to keep our work separate and independent. We can both become the other's assistant, but we do not participate in the other's work in terms of creative process or independence.

JS: What was your work like at that time?

SY: In the early 1980s, I was a student in the Chinese painting department, Zhejiang Academy of Fine Arts that was still quite traditional, and it took me some time to get beyond this training. At first I began doing anti-traditional experiments on paper, until I became aware of the limits of this approach. I did some other experiments in writing, drafting a few articles that had the flavor of "new short stories." Finally I threw down my pen and picked up the hammer, making the work *Water Bed* that was shown in the UCCA's " '85 New Wave" exhibition, moving from the two-dimensional surface into three-dimensional space.

JS: You moved to France in the 1980s. Your work reflects your immigrant experience, linguistic changes, and cultural struggles. Have these changes had any impact on your working method?

SY: Leaving China was quite a shock to my system. I remember it vividly, the sixteen-hour flight, landing in somewhere completely changed. People of my generation grew up in a completely closed environment, knowing absolutely nothing of the world beyond. I was shocked because I was not prepared, but only shock brings knowledge. This utter shift of cultural background forced me to spend three or four years just trying to understand my own position. This shift of background brought some new questions to the fore: "the other," "identity," "language." Facing new questions had quite an impact on my way of thinking.

When language proved an obstacle, art helped me to jump this boundary, so in my earliest works from France the form of the human tongue appears repeatedly, a symbol for language. The first work I made in Paris, *Perdre sa salive*, I did in a private basement. I made nine tongues out of ice, reaching outward from the columns and the ceiling. They were supported by knives, so when the ice melted, the knives shone through, a transposition of form.

JS: Your work *A Morning in the World* restructures traditional Chinese roofs. Is this work a memento of your hometown, placing it directly into a Western gallery context?

SY: My works are often fragments of my daily life, things that meant something to me at one time or place. I often use these things to stand for things that I want to say, placing them in these transformed contexts each time I am given an opportunity, with the hope that they can be useful to others. I become a creator, and do not merely remain an observer.

A Morning in the World is a memento of home and childhood made in a foreign place. This memory closes in on itself like the traditional Chinese roofs, visible but untouchable. I like to create incongruous scenes, to bring things from the past into the present, and to push the present back toward the past. This is what art can accomplish, finding its charm in the distance.

JS: Does this work, like other works of yours, touch upon questions of identity even as it explores the question of global migration?

SY: Yes. I have borrowed the form of a traditional four-walled, doorless roof to talk about the question of migration, creating enclaves each cut off from the other, each stopping at one or another past era. It's like in European cities, you have Chinatown, Little Italy, Little India, the Jewish Ghetto···　each consciously separating itself from the larger environment, trying to create an "old space" amidst this "new space." These "little spaces" fall under the "big space," and yet they have no connection to it. I once asked: "Is immigration turning your back on one space, or is it occupying another? I speak what was the mother tongue of my land at the moment I left it, but that language has changed, and I am stuck in the past."

JS: In your piece *Yellow Sofa*, Louis XV chairs are covered with traditional Chinese cloth. Is this a way of connecting Western or French history to China, as a way of reversing this French historical narrative, or Chinese history, or Chinese women's history?

SY: There is a proverb: "Beggars travel with all their luggage." An immigrant's "cultural baggage" manages to stick together through the process of "floating." In my work, I have been using more and more images where objects from different cultures come together. *Yellow Sofa* is a reflection of my background. Another

work, *Uncomfortable Shoes*, uses the kind of shoes that used to cover Chinese women's bound feet and black peasant "cloth shoes" to spell out the sentence "Elles sont parties, pourtant elles n'ont nulle part où aller" as a way of expressing the common situation of women post-feminism. During the Qing [Dynasty], women's feet were bound as a way of turning them into "commodities" and keeping them at home. Under Mao, the "black cloth shoes" marked another extreme, as women were stripped of all individuality – devoid of aesthetic value, rendered social tools. I used these two kinds of "shoes" coming from opposite extremes to write out a sentence in French, not Chinese, as a way of saying that this is not merely a Chinese question, but a universal question among women today.

JS: Where is home for you?

SY: If you ask a fisherman, "Where is home?" he will point to his boat. If you ask a Jew, he can only say, "If it is under my feet, where is not home?"

JS: How do you see this form that appears in your different works of the bridge between two worlds?

SY: Objects that migrate between two places are neither one nor the other, like a "bridge." A bridge spans a long distance, but it is dangerous, and it sways. It goes back and forth, like a migrant. I like to use materials that have to do with bridges: water and ice.

The bridges I have made are all bridges that cannot be crossed. The first of these was on a river in the tiny Dutch city of Leerdam, called *Crossing the River and Destroying the Bridge.* For this work I strung beer bottles from the local brewery, and kept them afloat using recycling bins. As soon as someone crossed, all they had to do was pull a string, and the bridge would cease to exist. I made another bridge for the Spanish NMAC Foundation near a racetrack, which looked more like an obstacle for horses, made of Chinese and Arabic porcelain bottles mixed together. The railings crossed halfway, making the bridge impassable. Isn't this also the function of culture?

JS: Do you see your works having a connection to childhood memory? What does memory mean to you?

SY: Some of the early works I did in France touch on this theme of memory, because at that point I still had not connected to my new environment, so memory surrounded me like a personal atmosphere.

JS: How would you describe your work?

SY: Most recently I did a piece at Galerie Kamel Mennour in Paris called *Le degré zero de l'espace*. On the evening of the opening, I used ice to seal the two main doors between myself and the viewers, separating off a space for myself. I exited the space on the second day, after the ice had melted. This is one way of working: the artist refuses to talk about or explain her works, and instead forces the works to speak for themselves.

JS: You are famous for using everyday objects in your work, from milk bottles to pacifiers and thermometers. Why?

SY: I have never known if I really count as a professional "artist." Art seems like just one responsibility among the many responsibilities in my life, neither large nor small. Only after I finish all the assorted things I have to do each day can I free up a little time for "art." If I have many different "professions," then "artist" is the last among them. If these ordinary obligations surround me like the air I breathe, then how could my art do without them? The idea for a work of art comes so unpredictably, sometimes when I'm reading, or in the second when I touch an object.

JS: So this is what you mean when you say, "Art is reincarnation, a way of exposing the hidden languages of things, of making the useless useful, and the useful useless, and this is what I want to do"?

SY: I said this, but what I meant was that people give artists a kind of "special power" that allows them to judge things based not on ordinary values, but which gives the things themselves new value. This is the responsibility of the artist.

JS: Why is your exhibition at UCCA called "Hurried Words"? Why must words be hurried?

SY: Speed is power, and so language can take on an unmistakable power. That's why revolutionary discourse employs slogans and commands like "strike down," "victory," "heads down," and "long live." Concise language equals a quick fist.

JS: In your piece *Hurried Words*, eighty hair dryers hang from the ceiling, each sticking out its "tongue" at a given interval. It's like something one would see at a party. Why did you choose to use these hair dryers?

SY: Tongues have appeared repeatedly in my work. Disconnected from the body, the tongue becomes a symbol of "discourse." The idea to use hair dryers to blow the tongues comes from a little toy I used to play with as a child, in Chinese called a "little tongue." Here a machine replaces human power. I first used blowers ten years ago, when I made a twelve-meter-long "forked tongue." It hung from a wall three or four meters tall and would inflate at intervals of four minutes. When the tongue blew up, it invaded the space, and when it shrank back down, it was kind of hiding. Every so often there would be this noisy sound of the tongue inflating, like someone speaking with a lisp, or unable to express their ideas. Perhaps this is a linguistic dilemma often encountered by immigrants. In this case, the eighty hair dryers give the feeling of a war of words or form of debate, and like debaters, they emit a lot of "hot air."

JS: **Your works possess a certain narrative power, as you use everyday objects to tell stories. In this piece *Landscape*, you also use a very ordinary object – the hairbrush – an object that is also quite private. But here you have put the hairbrush in a public space. The different hairstyles that appear come from different cultural backgrounds, but they inhabit the same big brush. Are you talking about the necessity and importance of putting different cultures together?**

SY: Everyday experience is always already "public" to some extent, like the way we all come into contact with the same mass-produced objects, which become "private" property only through use. I am taking these "privatized" objects, which are nonetheless mass-produced on assembly lines, and putting them back into the public space, perhaps as a way of evoking a shared experience. If you start with the simple notion that every day as we brush our hair, strands of hair will fall off and stick to the brush, then this brush is a public brush. In China from the 1950s to 1980s, all property was public: cafeterias, bathhouses, toilets, teacups, towels, kitchens, and so on. There was no such thing as private property. The only thing that could be private was "memory." So this brush resembles a public object, a public space. Everyone has left traces upon it, to the point where it looks like a crowd, or a forest. Different kinds of people and objects inhabit the same shared space.

JS: **In the opening of your solo exhibition "Le degré zéro de l'espace" in Kamel Mennour Gallery in Paris, you did a performance piece where you "froze" yourself in a room, and embroidered some text onto a "glass." This performance seems closely connected to the present work, in that both are about exchange. For people who live in "other" places, who have left the embrace of their mother tongue, language and exchange become problems. In your work this is a recurring problem. Can you talk about this a bit further?**

SY: The helplessness and resulting sense of being cut off from the world by virtue of not speaking the language was the most powerful and moving experience I had after leaving China. And in the twenty years that have passed, I have still not truly escaped from this position of "quiet remove." When you lack the confidence to talk to other people, you can only exist in this state, given over to internal monologues, trapped in the cycle of one's own self. My work *Le degré zéro de l'espace* is perhaps an unconscious exposé of this attitude, as well as a conscious gesture of self-seclusion. Ice separated personal space from public space, and I embroidered the sentence, "Personal space is stable, public space is floating, if one is calm, then the other is restless; when one starts to feel uncertain, the other finds its certainty…" I knew the wall of ice would melt, but when? Art is the only language capable of breaking through all cultural boundaries.

JS: There are many examples in your work of blowing up an everyday object, like this brush, or baby bottles, or thermometers. Why do you enlarge these objects? Is it in the name of magic or of poetry?

SY: Magic and poetry are inseparable. Magic is the *yang*, poetry the *yin*. But ultimately, expanding an object that you can hold in your hand to architectural proportions is a kind of magic. I think that after these proportions are altered, the very quality of the object also changes.

Take the thermometer; a little rod which can normally be stuck very easily into the body is blown up to three or four meters long, so that it evokes the golden cudgel of Sun Wukong [the Monkey King from *Journey to the West*]. Fish swim in the thermometer's belly and their movements change its reading. Moreover, the temperature of the fish is affected by changes in the temperature of the water in which they swim. I use this metaphor to talk about the ability of immigrants to adjust to new environments, so I named it *Poïkilotherme*.
I always use objects and events from my immediate surroundings to express myself.

JS: How do you see China today? As a Chinese woman artist, how do you feel?
SY: This era in China is one of seeking victory amidst the chaos. The art world is no exception – there are no rules of the game, and no one would bother to learn them even if they existed. This means that people dare to act, knowing that if they don't, someone else will. Every time I finish a work, I feel a pang of regret, but then I remember that I am both a Chinese artist and a woman artist, a double lack, so I'm allowed to make another.

(Translated from the Chinese by Philip Tinari)

沈远的词与物

Shen Yuan's
Words and Objects

郭晓彦
尤伦斯当代艺术中心首席策展人

GUO XIAOYAN
Chief Curator,
Ullens Center for Contemporary Art

Shen Yuan was born in 1959 in Xianyou, Fujian province, China. In 1982, she graduated from the Zhejiang Academy of Fine Arts (now re-named the China Academy of Art), and in 1989 she participated in the "China/Avant-Garde" exhibition at the National Art Museum of China. The next year, she moved to Paris. At that time, her most important work to date was *Water Bed*, which analyzed and criticized the social and political situation from her unique perception and intuitive perspective. After leaving China, the experience of cultural isolation and identity formation became a new starting point, and a new chapter in her work unfolded, drawing on ideas of cultural identity, historical memory and linguistic transformation in a complex new environment. In 1990, she began to draw attention in Paris and soon began an international career.

Shen Yuan is among the most outstanding and accomplished female artists of contemporary China. Her work often hovers between the ordinary landscapes of everyday life and the metaphors and transformations of language. It shifts between the registers of the magnificent and the masterly with a lithe, exquisite profundity. All the while, it also conveys complex bits of information and morsels of meaning.

In our modern experience, the possibilities allotted to humanity are proscribed by knowledge. This includes the regulatory power of thought, as both the entirety of one's knowledge, and one's drive toward propriety and correctness, as both an object of reflection and a transformation of that reflection. The goal of thought is to change one's existence, but paradoxically, this often occurs on the level of "non-thought." Thus

Foucault's idea is that "modern thought, from the beginning and at the deepest level, is a method of resistance." Thought transforms the other into the self. It is here that Foucault discovers that people exist inside the constraints of power, and this power functions to disperse people, divorcing them from their own origins. But this power is, in turn, none other than the power of people to exist. Thus, if there were no language, no connection between objects and words, we would be without connection to the larger world, without connection to history, unable to establish a realm for our own existence. In the long process of forgetting that appears before us, language is way of recovering "the form of time." Through the channel of our individual bodies (memories), it appears in the scope of a wide reading, as traces of personal narrative render the boundaries between individual and world ever more ambiguous, and thus render existence more clear. For the individual, language is not thought, nor wisdom, nor even truth. Rather, it is the "impromptu phrasing" of existence (per Barthes). On the other hand, language also carries a sense of history and illusion. Only through language can we confirm our own position relative to the world. In the 1994 Paris exhibition "Perdre sa salive", Shen Yuan's first solo outing outside of China, she showed work that she had made while abroad. It was work with a distinct connection to (Chinese) language, for in colloquial Chinese, the word for "tongue" (*shetou*) refers to an organ of both language and flesh. The Chinese set phrase *bai fei kou she*, which doubled as the show's Chinese title, refers to discussion (exchange) that bears no results. This work has everything to do with the artist's dislocation to another country, where language, and thus existence, was far from the realm of her motherland. It also brought to mind memories, summoned deep from the artist's unconscious, of despotic, guarded words. The exhibition featured several oversized, blood-red tongues, sculpted in ice and frozen around the columns of the exhibition space. The icy tongues melted over the course of the opening, dripping "saliva" slowly into metal pots and jars below. As the tongues melted away, they revealed the sharp knives that had been hidden inside them. Shen Yuan believes that, "because the word 'tongue' also means language, the melting away of the ice-tongue, an unlimited abuse of language, and the tongue itself comes to stand for the loss of language." When the tongue is invested with an active, complex function, it can become more violent than even the fist. *Perdre sa salive* was at the same time the artist's deep and detailed response to the loss that occurs when one is placed into an environment far from his or her mother tongue. As for the special properties of ice, Shen Yuan has her own opinion: It has a sturdy side, a soft side, and a fine, sensitive, feminine heart. Language shares these characteristics of fineness and sensitivity – it makes exchange possible, but at the same time, this often leads to subtle distortions which become huge misunderstandings.

The work *Hurried Words* shown at the Ullens Center for Contemporary Art was originally realized for Shen Yuan's 2008 exhibition in Paris. It is likewise a piece about language, with deep connections to her earlier works. The installation comprises eighty blowdryers, blowing out air that inflates the multi-colored "tongues" attached to their ends, and making them emit "hurried, quick words." Here,

the "language" they speak is both incomprehensible and deafening. And this is Shen Yuan's question: Having left behind the rich, nurturing realm of the mother tongue, how do we preserve the possibility, indeed, the ability, to speak our minds? How are we rendered lonely by such linguistic alienation? As the artist considers how the loss of language leaves us empty, she also exposes the power and the limits of language vis-à-vis description and translation of living realities. At the same time, how does the solid core of one's mother tongue stretch to encompass new elements from other languages, enabling new forms of thinking, reflection, and self-creation?

On the evening of her Paris opening, Shen Yuan left the crowd, closing herself off in a room behind two walls made of ice. On one side of the transparent divider, linguistic memory led her back to her far-off native tongue in a series of words that seemed ever farther from herself and her vocabulary. On the other side, she spent an entire night alone behind the ice wall, embroidering the questions that came into her mind in French, the language of her adopted country. For example, "Art allows me to transcend (linguistic) limitations in space and time," or "The tongue of an immigrant is like the tongue of a snake: contained and forked. The same tongue speaks two languages, and like the hissing of a snake, neither is clear." This work touches on another question that Shen Yuan has always pondered: Amidst complicated cultural realities, can we still believe in exchange? How can one use language to directly convey the complexities of one's life to the "other?" How can we tell "them" of our experiences? How does language take on different forms of comprehensibility, complexity, and mutability depending on context?

Shen Yuan once said that the artist's responsibility is to "endow objects with information." If her goal is indeed to give tongues to lifeless objects, we could say that she has endowed these objects with a usable, ready and varied way of communicating, be it oral or written. Even so, as in so many of her other works, this hope also expresses the uniqueness and the limits of language; perhaps only the visual can imbue the textual with meaning. "My interest always lies in transformations of form, this is the starting point for my work," she has said. The work *Landscape* which Shen Yuan created for the Ullens Center, bears a connection to a number of her other works that feature hair, works like *Three Person Sofa* (Graz, Austria, 1996), *In Threes and Fours, or in Knots* (for the exhibition "Parisien(ne)s", Camden Arts Centre/inIVA, London, 1997), and *Yellow Armchair* (Arnolfini, Bristol, UK, 2001). These works represent a series of considerations by the artist of the metaphorical potential hidden in the world beyond the body. We could even say that her pondering of bodily questions is made necessary by the transformations she has undergone.

In *Landscape* she has created here, the artist uses hair as a vehicle to discuss matters. But what does hair ultimately mean for people? The critic Wang Min'an has noted that: Hair and the body could be said to exist in a zero-sum relationship. Hair originates from the body, but the body systematically sheds it, seeing it as a superfluous or unnecessary object. Hair does not perform a vital function; it is useless, and thus cheap. At the same time, it has a seemingly endless capacity for regeneration, so it is never lacking. And yet the separation between hair and the body is absolute. It is not a painful separation, entailing neither spiritual angst nor physical pain. Rather, it is complete, tranquil, and never hurtful. It is ubiquitous, omnipresent, and prosaic. Hair strongly depends on the body for its genesis, but in its structure hair maintains but a fragile, contingent connection to the body.[1]

Coming from the body but also located beyond it, hair does not mark sexual differentiation, nor does it represent the "essence" of its subject. And yet it plays an important role in marking the cultural identity and temporality of its bearer. Hair length and style is a special symbolic marker of a person's external characteristics, and often, an index of one's subjectivity. In eras past, hair color was an intellectual signal that Chinese people could use to differentiate the ethnic other from the self: black belonged only to "us" Chinese, while blond, gray, red, and other colors were for "them." In Chinese culture there have been many derogatory epithets for foreigners based on hair color. Likewise, in the current moment of dyed hair, the ability to modify hair color has taken on a psychological characteristic, and the idea of hair as a site of one's unique qualities has given way to another in which hair, endlessly mutable, conveys the pressured and restless emotions of a later moment.

In Shen Yuan's work, the bristles of the hairbrush are topped with human hair that has fallen from real and different people. This object, familiar to all, becomes suddenly unfamiliar, bearing traces of

life even in its staggering lifelessness. In Shen Yuan's
world, "objects" carry different valences of meaning,
and choices that might appear arbitrary often take
on an unanticipated metaphorical heft. But what
vision of history do these objects intend to claim?
Do they seek to reclaim vanishing memories of life
and time? Or do they possess more of a political
significance – floating language, cultural exchange
amidst ever deepening globalization, the possibilities
(and impossibilities) of translation, the politics of
language?

Shen Yuan has expressed her hope that in revealing
the language hidden in objects, she can turn the
lifeless into the vital, waste into value, useful into
useless. She likes to make visible seemingly material
details, and these details in turn come to express
her sensitivities, her understanding of life and
the world, ever more aptly. In the two works that
make up this exhibition, we see the artist, as ever,
moving forward slowly amidst her own memory and
ponderings, intricately experiencing and considering
the special power of her work to prompt both
reflection and action.

(Translated from the Chinese by Philip Tinari.)

1   Wang Min' an, *Body, Space and Post-modernity*, Jiangsu People's Publishing House,
    2006, p. 68.

从他者的语言到跨文化性

From Alien Language to Trans-Culturality

索珂·法依－瓦卡里
巴黎第八大学美学副教授

SOKO PHAY-VAKALIS
Associate Professor in Aesthetics,
The University of Paris VIII

In our times, marked by the tragedies of history, societal mutations and dramatic political and ecological changes, the artists of migration display a dual cultural belonging as they question new trans-cultural practices and different forms of pluralist identity. Ever since her departure from China in 1990 (towards the West), Shen Yuan has never ceased to open up the debate on "hybridizing."She testifies to the slow and necessary mutual work of cultures that coexist, penetrate each other or borrow from one another. Her peculiar work, tainted with a sweetly subversive sense of *deprecation*, represents a significant force in the reorganization of global culture. Her creative dynamic shatters all prejudices and clichés of clashes of civilizations.[1] Going beyond local or national borders, her installations mix raw and temporary materials, sometimes even living organisms, and invite us into the discomfort inherent in all extraterritorial and trans-cultural rites of passage.

A Journey Towards Another Self

Having left her native country, Shen Yuan has centered her reflections and her art around the experience of restless wandering and of cultural and linguistic challenges and hurdles – hence embedding it in the historical and socio-economical realities of our time. She knows the suddenness and brutality with which exile befalls a person, bearing witness to her attachment to her roots which were forever shaken.[2] A world, a language, in which the emigrant lived, disappears, and confines him into solitude. The memory and strong impressions of the departure vividly remain with him. A lifetime is spent meditating on this moment of rupture when all shrinks to the essentials and one intimately experiences loss, the disappearance of one's roots and the absence of landmarks. *One Leaf, One Boat* (2001), a strange boat in the shape of a leaf, testifies to this experience. This precarious craft is made up of woks, tied together, filled with foods, spices and other oriental culinary products. Wherever they go, the Chinese always carry with them their tastes and flavors as precious goods or treasures. "Every exile carries his culture on his back", says Sarkis.[3] This feeling of uncertainty in adventure – as the leaf that lets itself be carried by the current – is reinforced by the melancholic voice coming out of the boat, that of Yang Yi, a young street singer whom the artist met in China. His songs speak of encounters, tell the tale of those who leave and try to rebuild their lives elsewhere, and the sometimes difficult, precarious conditions. Departure towards another is a journey towards another self.

In *Feel Just Like Fish in Water* (2001), exhibited in Bristol, a city in the United Kingdom famous for its blue glassware, Shen Yuan presents another variation on the theme of the boat, this time underlining the frailty, the will power, and the power of survival in exile. The installation shows a white desert sea upon which rests a small boat, fish bones and blue glass tableware, like archeological "leftovers,"relics of an ancient world. Meanwhile, inside the craft, fish swim in a little water. Through a game of inversions (the sea turned into a huge stretch of salt) and of detachment ("like a fish in the sea"), Shen Yuan shows creation, just like life, is as much a constant movement as it is a perpetual return from exile. She gathers the memory of places and experiences, but never stays ashore for too long. She lands for the length of an encounter, a "sharing of the sensitive,"[4] before taking off again, perpetually enriched from one space to another. For the one who has become a nomadic artist, the linguistic and spatial ordeal lies in both territories, as no return is possible. Indeed, the country of origin gradually becomes tainted with *strangeness*.

The Metamorphosis of Language

Even nineteen years after her arrival in France, Shen Yuan continues to work on linguistic and cultural "translation," to ponder the difficult and uncertain relationship with the Other. She captured these reflections in her exhibition and performance at the galerie Kamel Mennour in Paris in autumn 2008, *Le degré zéro de l'espace*. It was a homage to Roland Barthes who advocated succinct language, and simple forms as both a poetic and political effort.

On opening night, Shen Yuan withdrew from the public, making herself invisible and inaccessible behind two walls of ice, surrounded only by a few rudimentary objects (a wooden armchair, a table, thread and a blanket). On either side of the walls lay two worlds, separate, conflicting and impossible to superimpose. On one side, voices resonate from afar and are perceived as an incomprehensible mumble. On the other side, a vague silhouette can be made out through the melting ice. How long will the thaw take to allow for the "ice to break?"

This *ground zero* refers both to the temperature shock felt by the individual as he faces the difficulties of adaptation and to the refusal of interaction in an exhibition room, a place commonly dedicated to communication and financial flow. Isolating herself from the maddening crowd and the mumble of the world, Shen Yuan spent the night embroidering sentences onto the blanket. "To emigrate is to flee a space, or to try and occupy another space. I still speak my mother tongue from the time when I left. It has changed, but I have remained. Art allows me to get over these limits in time and space.""The language of migrants is like the tongues of snakes, wrapped up and split. The same tongue speaks two languages, and does not speak clearly, just like snakes hiss."

The latter sentence refers to a sound installation made up of eighty blow-dryers hanging from the ceiling by their electrical cords at different heights. Randomly, and at different times, they turn themselves on, the wind stretching out the multi-colored cloth tongues. These "words," brief and rapid, exhaust themselves through too much talking, and bear witness to the incomprehension and the inability to make oneself heard through the deafening noise. Every exile feels the pain of all those deprived of speech, precisely because it bestows legitimacy upon the being. The so-called "mother tongue," that is given to us at birth to tell the world, to describe the world, should therefore be immediately accessible. However, there is no device as complicated and impenetrable as language, building almost insurmountable barriers for the ears of a person who was not lucky enough to be "born within it." Therefore, acquiring the ability to speak in another's language constitutes an effort of thought, rebuilding and re-appropriation of the self after the uprooting. Shen Yuan has turned this experience of linguistic loss into a very powerful work: *Perdre sa salive* (*Losing One's Saliva*), exhibited in 1994 in a cave. Nine giant tongues of ice are displayed which, as they drip into spittoons, reveal their skeletons: nine big sharp knives. She plays on the multiple meanings of the "tongue," at once a means of communication and an organ, fleshy, gustative and sensual. It carries its own ambivalences, its metaphors (soft, sharp, hurtful) and expressions ("drooling like a dog" or, as the Chinese saying goes: "Is feeble the man who loses his saliva"). The transition from one image to another – the ice transformed into threatening knives – refers to the metamorphosis of the tongue. Exile then becomes, in sequence, a departure from the language passively received in one's roots, a reinvention of the power of words and the discovery of their autonomy.

The Discomfort of the In-between

The language and culture of exiles, which are both a territorial and psychological displacement, acquire a greater visibility, an acknowledgement via the translation of their emotional and cultural heritage. After all, isn't the original meaning of the word "translate" to "*pass over* ?" Through this lens, Shen Yuan invites each of us to experience the loss and shiftings of meaning. The discomfort[5] that stems out the disappropriation, the uncertainty of knowledge, is represented metaphorically by these strange bridges. Some are built with recycled glass bottles (see *Démolis le pont après la traversée de la rivière* [*Destroy the Bridge After Crossing the River*], 1997). Others are made of Chinese white porcelain vases showing blue landscapes, or ceramics of Arabic influence (*Pont*, [*Bridge*], 2004). Either way, they are impossible to cross. The crossing is somehow "hanging," suspended between the shores, mirroring the wrench and dilemma exiles experience,

between loyalty to their origins and allegiance to their adopted country. This "in-between" shows the ambivalence of a personal history caught in historical or cultural disjunction.

And yet, uncertainty is a notion feared by Western culture that likens the obscure and the hazy to clumsiness, mistake or even folly. Meanwhile, linguistic and cultural translation inherently works with a sense of uncertainty, "unachievable" because it circulates between two cultures, shedding light on their differences in order to express the world differently, in other forms, rhythms and colors. The relationship to the subject in its historicity alone will allow for the *understanding of sense*. That is why, even though the differences may sometimes be insurmountable, the encounter of the other enriches, and forms an essential subjective experience.

Thus, Shen Yuan undoes our sensorial habits as well as our expectations. From this barely perceptible experience, as divided as it is disorientating, she invites us to de-center the subject whose fragile equilibrium, between distanciation and identification,[6] is both constructed and deconstructed. The point is not to find the fusion point that would aim at resolving or surpassing the constraints, but to form an "alloy" of sorts that allows comprehension – taken together. This stance, albeit difficult and unstable, stems out of the un-shrinkability of cultures, but produces an energy of movement rendering us more attentive to the sharing of singular voices. In this perspective, "thinking the outside" or "thinking the in-between" would bring about the split, the difference and, this way, introduce the "becoming" as defined by Gilles Deleuze. "It is not one that becomes another, but a meeting of each other, a single becoming that is not common to both, since they have nothing to do with the other, but that is in between them, that has its own direction, a bloc of becoming, an a-parallel evolution."[7]

A Share of Un-translatable

Incomprehension and sometimes even uneasiness are often experienced when confronted with Shen Yuan's work, notably because of her use of live creatures, like fish. This stems out of our "ordeal," our "test of the other,"[8] faced with an art form channeling foreign aesthetic values as well as cultural habits and heritage. The difficulties in meeting the language and culture of the Other can indeed be summarized with the word "test"both in the sporting sense (a test match) and as "probation." Henceforth, the ambition of the artist would be to create works that would be seen, read or heard on both sides, all the while facing the paradox Paul Ricoeur described as an "equivalence without adequacy."[9] How can one make his own culture part with its share of *strangeness* ? How can a genuine dialogue start between oneself and the alien cum host.

It is to its inherent heterogeneity that the alien work owes its resistance to unequivocal interpretation. The creative act/process lies in the space between the un-translatability and the undetermined timing of the in-between. In this sense, the artist, as does the translator, takes both vows of fidelity and treason, proceeding to a rescue mission with the acceptance

of losses. Mourning an absolute culture is necessary to accept the dialectic gap between the proper and the alien. In *Essai sur l'exotisme* (*On Exotism*), Victor Ségalen had understood, a century ago, the risks of false alternatives, the dangers of a fusion that is nothing other than another form of appropriation and homogenization: "The great shortcuts of space, the collapse of barriers must be compensated, somewhere, by new walls and unforeseen gaps."[10]

As subversive as it may be, cultural translation is an aim, a vanishing point remaining open to the necessity of changes of historical and socio-cultural contexts. A very beautiful work by Shen Yuan, *Uncomfortable Shoes*, bears witness to this. A hundred little black slippers run along the walls, barely touching the ground. From a distance, we decipher a message "They[11] have gone, but they have nowhere to go." These shoes are reminiscent of different eras in China: the Qing dynasty, during which aesthetic codes imposed feet binding on women from a tender age; the Cultural Revolution that made style uniform (the same black color, with no distinction of age); and contemporary times, when migratory flows make thousands of women leave their countries in search of a better future but wind up in solitude and destitution. The lightness and grace of this installation are at the scale of the infinite exile and the tragedies of history.

Hybrid Caesuras

Through the use of metaphors, Shen Yuan also denounces the dramatic consequences of Chinese policies' radical decisions. *Ventre de Pierre* (*Womb of Stone*), a gigantic aquarium adorned with multi-colored, sculpted fish, represents the disaster brought about by the construction of the Three Gorges Dam. In *Errance im mortelle* (*Immortal Wandering*), she hung large pictures of her native village from a clothesline. The village, invaded and taken over by the discard and rubbish of a society struggling to regulate its ambition, its thirst for power and riches, has become unrecognizable. Underneath the line, strange birds, made of recycled materials, parade on a strip of crackled land, symbolizing the dried up ancestral tongue. Frenetic growth is not the solution to social imbalance and inequalities. On the contrary, these intense social mutations create exclusion and render even more precarious and difficult the life simple people or globalization left-outs. In order to survive, they can only count on themselves, and must be in constant search for new resources. In the southern province of China, rickshaws have disappeared from the streets, leaving in their place numerous traveling salespeople on bikes. *Tentacule* (*Tentacle*, 2008), presented at the Ullens Center for Contemporary Art (UCCA), is constructed from three old washed-out, seemingly used and abandoned blue rickshaw seats from which bikes detach and multiply. They remain, however, tied together with iron chains, like the jellyfish or the octopus and their numerous tentacles. Drivers no longer transport clients but go meet clients to sell cutlery, brooms, plants, birdcages, bug spray, or even toys and multi-colored balloons. Particularly sensitive to the evolution of the contemporary world, Shen Yuan suggests that we be more attentive to passage than to settlement, to prefer the process of translation and transition to sterile confrontations.

For her first solo exhibition in her native country, at UCCA, the artist chooses to focus on the great transformations and upheavals of our great restless metropolises through a hybrid and multi-layered work. *Paysage* (*Landscape*) is a massive eight-meter-long (Western) hairbrush – the use of the comb is much more widespread in Asia – made of traditional Chinese lacquered wood. This object, both intimate and banal evokes, by its shape, a boat as a metaphor for cosmopolitan "cities-world." Strands of hair attach themselves to the brush, get tangled up in the brush's orange tips like an abounding nature. From up close, you can tell the remarkable work of Shen Yuan, her attention to detail showing a great variety of hair: in color, gender, age, but also hairstyles, from the simplest to the most delirious. Symbols of life, of seduction, of strength and power in our civilizations, they define the relationship to the other as one of power or affection.[12] Whether straight, curly, permed, knotted or dyed, this hairs bears witness to the fecund mix of languages, cultures and religions.

Hence, former urban models have disappeared to give way to new realities. On one of the nozzles, the artist reproduced the cartography of Fuzhou, her native city, not for nostalgia's sake as much as to signify the importance of an affective memory[13] linked to a place, an affiliation, reflected in the hairdos made out of her father's hair. Memory, as the past-present *continuum*, becomes essential in a world in transition. The "trans"dynamic allows for the sharing of points of view and the recognition/acknowledgement of different senses and sensibilities. *Paysage* represents this very "third space"(urban), dear to Homi Bahbha: "Temporality out of sync with global and national cultures opens a cultural space – a third space – where the negotiations around incommensurable differences created tension particular to an existence at the edge."[14]

The essence of art wherein lies this capacity to "play" allows for creative transgressions where order and frontiers would be. It outlines articulations and reveals contradictions, creating a certain resistance to consensual uniformizsation and sterile nationalist fallback. Besides, in this "restructuring" of global culture, miscegenation should not be understood as a "collage" or a melting pot, but as the encounter of two images where, in the space of friction between cultures, something can be born. Without discrepancy, there can be no construction of shape.

Our world to be built would prefer a "plural otherness" that would simultaneously preserve several cultures.[15] Hence, going through the ordeal, the test of disappropriation and self de-centering would allow for the welcoming of the alien Other, the other not as a "conquest" (that would have placed the subject in a position of "power/knowledge") but as a "discovery." It is in this uninterrupted movement, made of "brightened" restless wandering, that Shen Yuan finds her creative resources. Her trans-cultural art would abolish the rigid opposition between East and West for a better understanding of the social, political and ecological transformations of the globalized era. Away from any claim to a Chinese artistic identity, Shen Yuan has never ceased to work within a space *in the making* in which each and everyone could redistribute the possibilities between art and life. Today, the challenge would be to define

an ethic to cultural translation that would no longer aim for the greater integration or assimilation of the other (for each subject is different in its historicity), but the construction of *a living-together* with the right to difference in equality and tolerance.

1 Voir E. W. Saïd, *L'Orientalisme, l'Orient crée par l'Occident* (1978), Paris, Seuil, 2005, p. 358.

2 Voir Shmuel Trigano, *Le temps de l'exil* (2001), Payot & Rivages, Paris, 2005, p. 17-19.

3 Voir mon article, "Mémoire et oubli: les figures du silence chez Sarkis," in *Art Absolument*, n° 5, juin 2003, p. 38.

4 J'emprunte l'expression à Jacques Rancière, *Le partage du sensible, esthétique et politique*, Paris, La fabrique-éditions, 2000.

5 Voir Homi K. Bhabha, *Les lieux de la culture* (1994), Paris, Payot, 2007, pp. 40-41.

6 Ibid, p. 33.

7 Gilles Deleuze, *Dialogues*, Paris, Flamarrion, coll, champs, 1996, p. 13.

8 Antoine Berman, *L'Épreuve de l'étranger*, Paris, Gallimard, 1984, pp. 15-16.

9 Paul Ricœur, *Défi et bonheur de la traduction*, in *Sur la traduction*, Paris, Bayard, 2004, p. 14.

10 Victor Segalen, *Essai sur l'exotisme*, Œuvres complètes, Paris, Laffont, Coll. Bouquins, 1995, p. 772.

11 "Elles", female, ndlt.

12 Voir *Chevelure*, in Philippe Seringe, *Les Symboles*, Genève, Helios, 1988.

13 Shen Yuan a plusieurs fois travaillé sur les métaphores des cheveux comme symboles de la vie, de la mémoire et de la solidarité, notamment dans *Three Armchairs* (1996), *In Threes and Fours or in Knots* (1997), *Hair Salon* (2000) ou plus récemment *Paysage* (2009).

14 Homi K. Bhabha, op. cit., p. 332.

15 François Laplantine, et Alexis Nouss, *Métissages, de Arcimboldo à Zombi*, Paris, Pauvert, 2001, p. 224.

简历

Biography

1959 年 5 月 26 日出生，福建，仙游
自 1990 年工作和生活在巴黎

个展

2009　沈远：急促的话语 / 尤伦斯当代艺术中心，
　　　北京，中国
2008　空间的零度 / 卡枚·蒙鲁尔画廊，巴黎，法国
2007　沈远 / A 艺术中心，温哥华，加拿大
2005　沈远 / 博蒙 & 公共画廊，卢森堡
2003　沈远 / 纽廷根艺术中心，德国
2001　沈远 / 蓝外套艺术中心，利物浦，英国
　　　沈远 / 阿尔隆非利，布里斯托尔，英国
　　　一个世界的早晨 / 切生海尔画廊，伦敦，英国
　　　沈远 / 英国法兰西学院，伦敦，英国
2000　在地下，有个天空 / 柏尔尼艺术中心，伯尔尼，瑞士
1999　歧舌 / 九州当代艺术中心，日本
1994　白费口舌 / "V&V" 协会主办，巴黎，法国瑞士

群展

2010　改造历史 / 2000-2009 的中国新艺术，国家会议中心，
　　　北京，中国
　　　世界的艺术 / 世博轴雕塑展；交叉小径的城市，
　　　上海，中国
2009　游戏时间—漫步圣日尔曼 / 巴黎，法国
　　　蹦床 / 在蓬皮杜收藏展"她"的展览期间展示，
　　　巴黎，法国
2008　领域 2008 / 世常青画廊－磨坊，巴斯．乐．
　　　夏德尔，法国
　　　我们的未来，尤伦斯基金会收藏展 /
　　　尤伦斯当代艺术中心，北京，中国
　　　艺术季节 / 中国美院，杭州，中国
2007　'85 新潮 / 尤伦斯艺术中心，北京，中国
　　　Global Multitude / 2007 欧洲文化之都，卢森堡
　　　第 52 届威尼斯双年展 / 中国馆，威尼斯，意大利
2006　第 5 届深圳水墨展 / 深圳，中国
　　　无论我们去哪里 / 当代摄影博物馆，米兰，意大利
　　　光州双年展 / 光州，韩国
　　　艺术的力量 / 大皇宫，巴黎，法国
2005　广州三年展 / 广州博物馆，中国
　　　超"凡"脱"俗" / 沪申画廊，上海，中国
　　　愚公移山 / 中法文化年，广东，中国
　　　墙 / 世纪坛，北京，中国
　　　桥下 / 岸边，卡西诺，卢森堡
　　　别碰白种女人：多样化及解放下的当代艺术 / 蛋堡，
　　　那不勒斯，意大利
2004　奥德赛 / 2004，上海画廊，上海，中国
　　　白夜 / 当代公共艺术组织，巴黎，法国
　　　别碰白种女人：多样化及解放下的当代艺术 /
　　　桑德托 - 瑞波德哥基金会，都灵，意大利
　　　利物浦双年展 / 利物浦，英国
　　　金门当代艺术碉堡博物馆：18 个艺术家个展 /
　　　金门，中国台湾
　　　自然化艺术 / 蒙当美迪当代艺术基金会，西班牙
　　　东南以西 / 西南以东 /
　　　朗格多克 - 胡希容地方现代艺术中心，塞特，法国
　　　道与魔 / 里昂当代艺术博物馆，里昂，法国
　　　找不着北 / 阿尔松别墅，尼斯，法国
　　　天下：中国古代及当代艺术展 /
　　　尤伦斯基金会收藏，安特卫普当代艺术博物馆，
　　　安特卫普，比利时

2003　新地带：中国艺术 / 扎切塔当代艺术画廊，华沙，波兰
　　　谢素美：沈远 / 博蒙公众画廊，卢森堡
2002　交点 / 金沙萨 - 南特，金沙萨美术学院，
　　　南特美术学院，法国
　　　圣保罗双年展 / 圣保罗，巴西
2000　巴黎作为中转站 / 巴黎市立现代艺术博物馆，法国
　　　费乌里 乌索 2000 / 比斯卡拉，意大利
　　　大陆漂移 / 列日，比利时
　　　2000 诺言 / 贝尔维尔广场，巴黎，法国
　　　家 / 上海，中国
1999　世界不平行 / 勒蒙高等艺术学院，勒蒙，法国
　　　半边天 / 奥芬堡，德国
　　　移动中的城市 5 / 海乌尔画廊，伦敦，英国
　　　艺术与建筑 / 亚洲美术画廊，柏林，德国
　　　一个世界的早晨 / 爱利可·德柏画廊，巴黎，法国
　　　移动中的城市 4 / 路易斯安娜现代艺术博物馆，丹麦
1998　移动中的城市 3 / PS1，纽约，美国
　　　空地 / 坎特伯雷艺术和设计学院，坎特伯雷，英国
　　　半边天 / 妇女博物馆，波恩，德国
　　　移动中的城市 2 / 波尔多当代艺术博物馆，
　　　波尔多，法国
　　　空地 / 鲁昂美术学院，鲁昂，法国
1997　移动中的城市 1 / 维也纳 SECESSION，
　　　维也纳，奥地利
　　　玻璃杯 / 莱尔丹玻璃艺术节，莱尔丹，荷兰
　　　不确定的快感 / ART BEATUS 画廊，温哥华，加拿大
　　　巴黎人 / 卡姆登艺术中心，伦敦，英国
1996　包容与排拆 / 格拉茨，奥地利
1995　人的跌落 / 3 房和 1 厨房画廊，波里，芬兰
　　　费尔巴赫三年展 1995 / 维也纳当代美术馆，奥地利，
　　　巡回地点，斯图加特
1994　梭 / 贝塔林艺术之家，柏林，德国
1989　中国 / 现代艺术展 / 中国美术馆，北京，中国
1986　福建美术展 / 福建美术馆，福州，中国
1984　福州妇女艺术展 / 福建美术馆，福州，中国

Born in 1959 in Xianyou, China.
Lives and works in Paris since 1990.

SELECTED SOLO EXHIBITIONS

2009 Shen Yuan: Hurried Words / UCCA, Beijing, China
2008 Le degré zéro de l'espace / Galerie Kamel Mennour, Paris, France
2007 Shen Yuan / Centre A, Vancouver, Canada
2005 Galerie Beaumontpublic / Luxembourg
2003 Shen Yuan / Kunstverein Nürtingen, Germany
Beauty room 5 / Beauty room gallery, Paris, France
2001 Shen Yuan / Bluecoat, Liverpool, UK
Shen Yuan / Arnolfini, Bristol, UK
Un Matin du Monde / Chisenhale Gallery, London, UK
Shen Yuan / French Institute, London, UK
2000 Sous la terre / il y a le ciel, Kunsthalle de Berne, Switzerland
1999 Diverged Tongue / Project Gallery at CCA Kitakyushu, Japan
1994 Perdre sa salive / Organized by "Vices & Vertues", Paris, France

SELECTED GROUP EXHIBITIONS

2010 Reshaping History / Chinart from 2000-2009 / China National Convention Center , Beijing , China
Art for the World (The Expo) - World Expo / The city of forking paths, Shanghai, China
2009 Play time-parcours Saint Germain / Paris, France
Trampolines / exhibited during "Elle", collective show of the museum collection , Centre George Pompidou, Paris , France
2008 Sphères 2008 / GalleriaContinua / Le Moulin, Boissy le Châtel, France
Our Future, The Guy & Myriam Ullens Fontation collection / UCCA, Beijing, China
Artseason / The China Academy of Art, Hangzhou, China
Rouge gorge, le trait d'esprit, Le Forum, le Blanc-Mesnil, France
2007 '85 New Wave / The Birth of Chinese Contemporary Art, Ullens Center for Contemporary Art , Beijing 798, China
Global Multitude / European Capital of Culture 2007, Luxembourg and Greater Region
52th Venice Biennial / Chinese Pavilion, Venice, Italy
2006 5th International Ink Painting Biennial of Shenzhen / Shenzhen, China
Wherever We Go / Museo di Fotografia Contemporanea, Milan, Italy
Gwangju Biennial / Gwangju, Korea
La force de l'Art / Grand Palais 2006, Paris, France
2005 Guangzhou Triennal / Guangdong Museum of Art, Guangzhou, China
From Mundane to Extraordinary / Shanghai Gallery of Art, Three on the Bund, Shanghai, China
Fools Move Mountains / France-China, Guangdong province, China
Wall / The Millennium Altar, Beijing, China
Sous les ponts / Le long de la rivière, Casino, Luxembourg
Don't Touch White Woman - Contemporary Art Between Diversity and Liberation / Castel Dell Ovo Napoli, Naples, Italy
2004 Odyssée 2004 / Shanghai Gallery, Shanghai, China
Nuit blanche / Art Public Contemporain, Paris, France

Don't Tounch White Woman-Contemporary Art Between Diversity and Liberation / The Fondazione Sandretto Re Rebaudengo of Torino, Italy
Liverpool biennial / Liverpool, UK
18 Solo Exhibitions / Bunker Museum of Contemporary Art, Kinmen, Chinese Taiwan
Arte y naturaleza lil / Montenmedio Arte Contemporaneo, Cadiz, Spain
A l'ouest du sud de l'est / Centre Régional d'Art Contemporain Languedoc-Roussillon, Sète, France
Le moine et le démone / Musée d'Art Contemporain de Lyon, Lyon, France
A l'ouest du sud de l'est/A l'est du sud de l'ouest / Villa Arson, Nice, France
All Under Heaven: Ancient and Contemporary Chinese Art / The Collection of the Guy & Myriam Ullens Foundation, MuHKA (Museum of Contemporary Art Antwerp), Antwerp, Belgium
2003 New Zone- Chinese Art / The Zacheta Gallery of Contemporary Art, Warsaw, Poland
Su-mei tse / transports croisés / air de mode / Shen Yuan / Galerie Beaumontpublic, Luxembourg
2002 Rond-point / Kinshasa-Nantes, Kinshasa School of Fine Arts - Ecole des Beaux-Art de Nantes, France
Sao Paulo Biennial / Sao Paulo, Brazil
2000 Paris pour escale / Musée d'Art Moderne de la Ville de Paris, Paris, France
Fuori uso 2000 / Pescara, Italia
Continental Shift / Liège, Belgium
Promesses pour les années 2000 / Espace Belleville, Paris, France
Home / Shanghai, China
1999 Le monde non parallèle / Ecole Supérieure des Beaux-Arts du Mans, France
The Half of the Sky / Offenburg, Germany
Cities on the Move 5 / Hayward Gallery, London, UK
Art & Architecture / Asian Fine Art Factory, Berlin, Germany
Un Matin du Monde / Galerie Eric Dupont, Paris, France
Cities on the Move 4 / Louisiana Museum of Modern Art, Denmark
1998 Cities on the Move 3 / P S 1, New York, USA
Terrain Vagues / The Herbert Read Gallery Kent Institute of Art & Design, Canterbury, UK
The Half of the Sky / Frauen Museum Bonn, Germany
Cities on the Move 2 / CAPC Museum, Bordeaux, France
Terrains Vagues / Ecole régionale des Beaux-Arts, Rouen, France
1997 Cities on the Move / The Vienna Secession, Vienna, Austria
Het drikglas / Stichting Leerdam Glasmanifestatie, Leerdam, Holland
Uncertain Pleasure / Art Beatus Gallery, Vancouver, Canada
Parisien(ne)s / Camden Arts Centre/inIVA, London, UK
1996 Stirischer herbst 96 / (Inclusion - Exclusion), Reinighaus, Graz, Austria
1995 The Fall of the Man / Three Room and a Kitchen, Pori, Finland
Triennial Fellbach 1995 / Südwest LB Forum Stuttgart, Stuttgart, Germany
1994 Le Shuttle / Künstlerhaus Bethanien, Berlin, Germany
1989 China/ Avant-Garde / China National Art Gallery, Beijing, China

1986 Exhibition of Fine Arts of Fujian / Museum of Fine Arts of Fujian, Fujian, China
1985 Exhibition of Women of Fuzhou / Museum of Fine Arts of Fujian, Fujian, China

图书在版编目（CIP）数据

沈远：急促的话语：中英对照 / 尤伦斯当代艺术
中心，一石文化编. 一上海：上海人民出版社，2010
    ISBN 978-7-208-09398-0

    Ⅰ. ①沈… Ⅱ. ①尤…②一… Ⅲ. ①造型（艺术）
一作品集一中国一现代 Ⅳ. ①J06

中国版本图书馆CIP数据核字（2010）第122264号

责任编辑　张铎
特约编辑　史建　马健全 / 一石文化
装帧设计　吐毛球平面设计

世纪文景

沈远：急促的话语
尤伦斯当代艺术中心　一石文化 编

出版　　世纪出版集团　上海　人民出版社
　　　　（ 200001 上海福建中路193号www.ewen.cc ）
出品　　世纪出版股份有限公司　北京世纪文景文化传播有限责任公司
　　　　（ 100027 北京朝阳区幸福一村甲55号4层 ）
发行　　世纪出版股份有限公司发行中心
印刷　　北京雅昌彩色印刷有限公司
开本　　787×1092　1/16
印张　　6.75
字数　　189,000
版次　　2010年8月第1版
印次　　2010年8月第1次印刷
ISBN　　978-7-208-09398-0/J·184
定价　　198.00元

版权所有，翻版必究。